MAKE LIFE COLORFUL

Book by Omid Vafa

Pursuing the Creative Dream
Without Giving Up on Hope

Title: Make Life Colorful

Subtitle: Pursuing the Creative Dreams without Giving Up on Hope

Author: Omid Vafa

Foreword by: His Holiness Dalai Lama

DEDICATION PAGE

To my Father Mansour and Mother Mahnaz
with Respect, Love and Gratitude

His Holiness Dalai Lama

THE DALAI LAMA

FOREWORD

Human beings are fundamentally all the same—physically, mentally, and emotionally. Together, we inhabit this Planet Earth. We face many challenges that could be avoided if we were to nurture a sense of the oneness of humanity and treat our fellow human beings with warm heartedness and loving kindness.

Every year, due mainly to intercommunal conflicts, hundreds of thousands of people are displaced from their homes and communities and are forced to seek refuge in a foreign land. The pain of leaving their homeland is devastating, and the uncertainty of finding a safe haven can be overwhelming.

The book, *Making Life Colorful* by Dr. Omid Vafa, demonstrates that despite many challenges, his ability to survive and lead a meaningful life in a foreign country was made possible largely by the kindness of others. Out of appreciation for their generosity, and recognizing the importance of extending the same warm heartedness to others in need, he founded a Charitable Foundation. I hope that readers of this book will find the author's experiences inspiring.

24 May 2022

Acknowledgements

Writing and publishing a book is much harder than one can ever imagine, and more rewarding than I had expected. No scholarly work is an entirely individual enterprise and mine is certainly not an exception. Number of scholars, reviewers, and friends have assisted me in various ways during preparation of this book.

It took me a few years to find the time, the right place, and the right person to work on this project with. I am grateful to *Whitney Bolibol* for her diligent assistance in completing this book. Her professionalism and commitment was admirable and rewarding.

Several great friends and colleagues each provided invaluable counsel, support and contributed to shaping this book to come alive. Special thanks to O.J Salari, Andi Salari, Houston Ross, Terrence Farnsworth, Omid Samimi, Sam Ohta, Sia Vali, Lars Godzik, Nadim Missaghian, Hooman Shirazi, Robert Morgan, Jonathan Miller, Ramin Aryan, Aaron Kleiman, Edmond Sam, Saeid Yazdanmehr, Lionel Martin, A.K, Lucas Oliver Frost, Rolf Alfred Lumpe, Patricia Bader-Johnston, Michael Graffagna, John Kostopoulos. I am genuinely grateful for their encouragement and thoughts in shaping this book.

To all the individuals I have had the opportunity to lead, be led by, or watch their leadership from afar, I want to say thank you for being the inspiration and source for the professional life I have built. I cannot thank more and certainly to those who supported and devoted their passion and professionalism to Runway for Hope foundation which has been the main part of my life. Their motivation and enthusiasm kept us growing and shining.

Finally, my greatest debt of gratitude is due to the very best father and mother who gave me life and unconditional love, who supported and protected me all the way to be a worthy child. With their wisdom and lifetime guidance I would not be here willing to survive and appreciate the true value of life. My very warm-hearted sister Arezoo who brought us so much joy since the day she opened her eyes to this world, I am so proud of what she has been through and achieved in life. First and foremost, I am grateful to them for their endless prayers, compassion, inspiration, and sacrifices. It is because of their efforts and encouragement that I have a legacy to pass on to my family where one didn't exist before.

The rare occasions when one stops and acknowledges one's debt to others are humbling but rewarding. What a blessing to be surrounded by so many good people! Indeed, without their support and endless sincere friendship and love this journey would not be completed at all. I deeply thank everyone and hope these pages are some repayments.

About The Author

Omid grew up in numerous multicultural communities around the world, being fortunate to travel to over 70 countries and live in more than 12. During his childhood, he lived in Afghanistan (1976-1980) where his father was stationed as a diplomat from Iran. In the later years of his stay in Afghanistan, Omid survived 4 coups d'état, including a Soviet Union invasion before moving back to Iran. He moved back to his home country during a time of chaos. It was the final month of the Pahlavi empire and Iran was undergoing political shifts due to the Iranian Revolution (1979) and war with Iraq (1980).

Throughout his 5 years return to Iran, Omid experienced the Iran and Iraq war. With the eruption of war and the persecution Baha'is were facing after the Iranian Revolution, he had no other choice but to flee. Omid left his family behind before turning 16 in hopes of a brighter future. He prevailed on another perilous journey during his time as a refugee in Pakistan for over 2 years (1985-1988) before getting the opportunity to start a new life in Canada. He lived there for just over a decade without having to worry for his physical safety. Following his life in Canada, U.S, Australia and the UK, Omid moved to Japan (2005) and began immediately searching for ways to contribute his knowledge and experience to the Japanese community.

Among some active roles as an advisor in the corporate world, Omid is a philanthropist, entrepreneur, and public speaker, giving talks on a variety of topics on entrepreneurship, fashion and education to youth and various interest groups/associations, athletes and corporate.

Author's Timeline

AFGANISTAN - 3 Coup
d'états and Soviet Union
invasion 1979

IRAN and IRAQ War

Migration to CANADA

| 1976–1980 | 1979–1980 | 1980–1985 | 1985–1988 | 1988–1998 |

IRAN - Revolution Period

Refugee Camp - PAKISTAN

CONTENTS

FORWARD

M*ake Life Colorful* is a unique approach to the values of life, family, and the directors of our lives, helping us shape our lives. This book inspires change through stories from the author's life that many can connect with. *Vision, Hope, Courage,* and *Paying it Forward* are four important pillars outlined in the book. Together, they are the guidelines to better understanding life's values and leading a more colorful life.

This book challenges the bleak, hard-working structure of society by asking the fundamental question: "How can we live life colorfully?" This question is about guiding the youth to having a stronger, more prepared future where they utilize their talent to create a brighter world, along with challenging the current generation to think outside of the box and look within themselves to see what is missing. This question challenges you to not only think within, but also towards the world without. Think of all the people in your life, your neighbors, family, and community, strangers you have yet to meet, and then try to think of them all as one. No differences, no bias or judgment, just as individuals trying to live a colorful life. How can we create a unity of color and bring back the moments we missed and deserved to have in life?

This book creates dialogue between where we are in life and where we want to go. Just as colors are all different and beautiful, so are we as individuals. However, we all have the opportunity to come together and turn our individuality into something truly stunning. It is for this reason that we need to help one another, have more empathy, be there for each other, and stop isolating people based on their differences. *Make Life Colorful* isn't just an inspiring work of art that follows the author's life of struggle and striving. It is a heart-felt and complex narrative that delves into *why* these pillars are an integral part of life and how to utilize *Vision, Hope, Courage,* and *Paying it Forward* to create the life you want and not the life you have settled for.

Omid Vafa, the author, grew up in a Baha'i household where his father was a diplomat during the last years of the Shah of Iran. His father was stationed in Afghanistan where they lived for a time before unrest and turmoil arose. Omid and his family survived 4 coups d'états, including a Soviet Union invasion before moving back to Iran. From childhood, Omid's life has been a rollercoaster of struggling, change and an uncertain future. In Afghanistan, he wondered if he would survive tomorrow and live to see a brighter future. When he moved back to Iran, life wasn't much easier. Iran was also in a state of change and chaos due to the recent Iranian Revolution. Throughout his pre-teen and teenage years, Omid was forced to think long and hard about where he existed in the world and within Iranian society as a Baha'i. What did the future hold for him and how could he make his life colorful despite all the suffering happening in and around his life?

Though Iran was mainly a Muslim state, the Baha'i faith was originated in Iran in 1863 by Baha'u'llah. It is a minority religion that has faced ongoing persecution. Universal peace upheld by a world government, the oneness of humanity, and the essential harmony of science and religion are just a few principles that the Baha'i faith is built on. There are over 6 million Baha'is in the world, over 180 countries. It has been a source of both hardship and reprieve for Omid in his years.

However, struggle and suffering never stopped Omid from having vision and chasing after his dreams. As he grew up, Omid found himself being more curious about the beliefs he practiced and wondered how the principles he learned were so different from the world he lived in. Between experiencing the Iran and Iraq war and the persecution Baha'is were facing, Omid had no other choice but to flee for his life, leaving his family behind when he was 15. Barely a teenager and years from being a young adult, Omid had to face adulthood all on his own and learn how to survive by himself. Along with others fleeing for their life, he trekked through the desert and mountains for the span of a week with no food and no water in order to reach the neighboring country, Pakistan, and to join other refugees who also fled for their lives.

Even after his perilous journey, the refugee period was scarcely any better. He stayed at the camp for two years, surviving on the bare necessities and waiting every day for a chance at a better life. After two long years, Omid was finally granted entry into Canada where he was given the opportunity to restart his life. However, he was barely an adult and alone in a country he barely knew. Omid toiled away at creating a better and more stable life for himself with his own two hands. It would be thirteen years before he saw his family again, but the life he had created in that time was something he worked and struggled hard for.

The author's journey in life was one of great struggle and hardship, but using what he learned in life, Omid hopes to impact those facing their own struggles. *Make Life Colorful* follows these stories, going into transparent detail about the author's thoughts, surroundings, and how he fought and strove to make a better life.

Vision is something that festers inside all of us, something that we nurture at a young age. It is what leads us to the future and sets us on our path. *Hope* is what encourages our vision to blossom into fruition. Hope is instilled within us by those around us that we respect and care for. *Courage* is the strongest when paired with hope. It is what we need when we face obstacles that threaten our livelihood, our hope, and our vision; it is what we need when we fall down. Finally, after we have reached a point in our journey where we are ready to give back and contribute to society, it is important to remember the trials you've gone through and the people who've helped you. *Paying it Forward* is an important key in completing the cycle of life and making life colorful.

Make Life Colorful is broken up into four parts that follow the four elements of living a colorful life. Each part has respective chapters that delve into deeper understanding of each pillar, motivating the readers to want to implement these elements into their own life. At the end of each section will be interactive questions and creative content to keep the readers engaged and stay motivated throughout the book. These interactive activities will expand at the end of the book where more reflective and meaningful activities will be available for the readers to utilize in order to start their own journey to a more colorful life.

The first part of *Make Life Colorful* is titled "Dream Big - Start Near." This section focuses on the element of "vision" and how vision is the foundation for the other elements to thrive. Vision is what each human nurtures at a young age; it stems from asking questions about the world around you and grows as your knowledge expands. This element in life isn't optional and we cannot choose to welcome or deny vision, it will come into our life regardless. It is our duty to nurture and harness the vision that grows within all of us.

In the first chapter of the section, we speak about the author's childhood and how his innocent questions about the poverty and hardship around him had expanded his vision over time. The curious childhood of the author is seen in very defining moments that stays with him throughout his adolescence. The questions he asks only grow as he ages, and his determination to do something about the vision he has is supported by the "directors" in his life.

In chapter two, we speak about the "directors" in life. These directors are the people in your life that motivate and encourage you to dream big and chase your goals. There are three major directors in life: family, friends, and mentors. They impact your life in various ways and different capacities. Sometimes it is through daily encounters while other times it is reading about or watching your favorite characters. In this section, we talk about the directors in the author's life and how they had supported him and helped nurture his vision when the questions he asked were too big to contain.

In contrast, not all directors in life are good. There are those who make you second guess yourself and doubt your vision. These directors feed off of your disheartenment and negativity, however, these people and their comments about your life don't need to be the reason you feel discouraged. The author talks about using the negative comments to fuel your drive and motivation. Do the best you can in order to show these people that they were wrong about you and your vision. As long as you believe in yourself and have good directors around you, you can achieve anything.

Even with a vision and directors to support your vision, life doesn't always go as planned. Chapter three outlines the changes that occur within our vision. As we grow as individuals and as life changes around us, so do our dreams and aspirations. There are things in life that no one can plan for. Whether you are faced with suffering, hardship, or life just gets in the way, it is okay to fail. Even if you fight and work toward your vision every day, there are situations that are beyond our control that prevent us from achieving our vision.

Vision isn't a singular dream we should hold onto for dear life. It is important that we nurture and foster many dreams, so that when one fails, we can continue onwards with another. Even if we have failed, we still learn from the work we've put in and from our mistakes. There is no use dwelling on what could have been when we can use our failure as an opportunity to start anew.

Everything in life has meaning and there is a reason behind it; success, failure, uncertainty, these are just elements that play into the grand spectrum of our life. Even after years of working towards his vision, the author, too, failed at completing one of his biggest dreams. Though it was frustrating and disappointing, there were things beyond his control that prevented him from achieving and eventually led to his failure. However, the author used his failure as a stepping stone to a brighter and better vision. Though he failed he was able to pick himself up and continue forward.

In the last chapter, chapter four, we talk about the important steps the reader should take to achieve and strive towards their own vision. Though everyone is different, and everyone fosters their own, unique, individual dream, it is important to realize that without a *plan, determination, keeping faith,* and *action,* working hard towards your dream and vision is a futile task. In this chapter we outline these four important steps, going into more detail about *why* they are important and what we can do to make sure we follow these steps. How we execute these four steps isn't as important as *doing*. As long as we focus, believe in ourselves, and have determination to become a better version of ourselves, that is all that matters.

At the end of this section, as we will see in the next three parts, there is a two-page interactive questionnaire that guides the readers through some of the important points covered in the chapters. This portion of the chapter allows the readers to really digest what they have read and interact with the book itself.

In part two, "Value Yourself - Appreciate Loved Ones" we delve into the second pillar of making life colorful: Hope. This section provides the readers with principal guidelines to building a strong supportive life. There are many guiding lists for the reader to refer to and very informative insights provided in each chapter within this section.

In the first chapter, we talk about the value of life and how easy it is for people to lose focus. With the progression of society, technology, and cultures, we are often distracted by the core values of life that add color to our lives. It is easy to fall onto the path of the materialistic, however, this doesn't lead to a full life. Giving back, remembering loved ones, and treasuring the small moments of happiness in your life is what will bring your life color. In this chapter, we list several methods on how to live a brighter and more colorful life before moving onto chapter two.

Chapter two and three, we talk about the people in our lives who give us hope. Though this may look different for everyone we also have people who instill hope in us. Our family is our closest allies and the ones that we turn to first for comfort and love. Chapter two outlines the importance of family, not just as children looking up to our parental figures, but as parents looking at their children.

Hope is a two-way street and though each parent can only give a certain amount of hope based on their unique, situational capacity, it is without a doubt that they are the ones trying their hardest to provide a bright future for their children. However, life situations can get in the way of hope between parents and children. As culture changes throughout each generation, so does our relationship with our family. It is imperative that we recognize how society has changed us and focus our attention on building or rebuilding strong and closer relationships with those who are near and dear to us.

Similarly, in chapter three, we speak about friends and how they are our second closest allies. While they are important directors to our vision, they are also the family we choose. We talk about different friendship zones and which friendships we should hold tightly. While friendship is essential to our hopes and dreams during our lifetime, it is harder to make friends as we get older. We give the readers tips on how to make and hold onto strong friendships, while also giving anecdotes about the author's friendships and how friends had played an important role in his life.

Chapter four is about happiness and the value of happiness. Although we strive towards our goals and are lifted up by the hope we are given by our friends and family, life is a constant struggle. We are perpetually fighting for a brighter and more colorful future that is often burdened by society and invisible pressures. Sometimes, it is hard to look for the rainbow on a rainy day, and in this chapter, we encourage the readers to look for small slices of happiness in everyday life. The grand accumulation of happiness cannot be forced, nor does it happen when you want it to. But by focusing on the small aspects of life that make us happy, we can begin to realize and learn what makes us truly happy.

The author has also faced many struggles and dark days in his life. In this chapter, the author talks about the struggles he has faced throughout his life that eventually led to one of the happiest moments of his life. Not everyone goes through the same hardships or struggles, but happiness can always be achieved. It is important to focus on today and what makes you happy here and now. You cannot change what happened yesterday and you don't know what tomorrow holds, but what you do today can have an impact on your tomorrow.

At the end of this chapter, we end with a small questionnaire before moving onto part three: "Strive and Take Off." This section represents the third pillar, *courage*, and it reads more as a memoir, though the life lessons shared translate into the third pillar of courage.

In the first chapter, we talk mainly about the author's childhood during his move between Afghanistan and Iran. The story about the author's father demonstrates how easy it is to lose hope and courage when faced with struggle and suffering. Being resilient isn't easy and there are times when we all struggle with the darkness that encroaches on our lives, however, the author points out that it is important to always remember that today is just temporary, and that tomorrow could hold a brighter future. Despite the struggles, we owe it to ourselves to push forward and have the courage to live another day.

The second half of the first chapter tells a different story about a refugee by the name, Salman. The author meets this man later in life and he resonates with the heart-breaking story of Salman. Here, we see the strength and courage it takes to have hope and to continue living when the world has taken everything from you. While this touching story isn't something many readers can relate to, the feeling of helplessness and defeat is something many of us know well. The author reminds us that just having hope or solely relying on courage will only get us so far in life. It is when we combine the two that we can transcend and live a more colorful life.

Chapter two transitions to an intimate retelling of the perilous journey the author had to embark on in order to become a refugee. This is the story of how hope and courage was created within the author. Hope with courage is built slowly and carefully, but it is during our darkest times when hope and courage shines the brightest. This chapter reminds readers that it is okay to feel helpless sometimes. It is normal to feel like your journey to happiness and comfort is never ending. However, in spite of the struggle, it is important to believe in yourself, hope for a brighter future, and have the courage to continue on.

In chapter three, the author shares his stories of being a refugee. He describes to the readers what it feels like to be a refugee and how, despite all that he went through, he still wasn't guaranteed security. Even so, we see how friendship plays a large role in the author's journey. Though he was without his parents, the friends he made at the refugee period influenced the man he became. They gave him courage and hope, even when the future was an antagonizing waiting game. Because the author had the courage to see his perilous journey through, he was able to meet so many amazing people who shared his suffering and his happiness. The transition between two worlds takes time, patience, and courage.

To make a more colorful future and live a colorful life, we cannot cower under the unknown. Though the future might be uncertain and scary, we need to have the courage to hope for a better tomorrow, and chapter four shows how the author was able to shine bright on his darkest days. Not every transition is an easy one, and the choice to make a change when your world has become dark, and bleak takes time and effort. Chapter four tells the story of the author's post-refugee. The author moved to Canada where everything was different, new, and full of hope.

This chapter elaborates on the author's vulnerability that readers can all connect with. When things in life change, we all second guess our vision, our hope, and our courage. Sometimes we fall into a darkness that is hard to get out of. However, the author shares his story of climbing out of the darkness and starting a new life all alone in Canada in his early twenties. It wasn't easy nor was it fast; it took time and effort for the author to make the change. In the end, his earnest strive towards a brighter future was rewarded by the reunion of his family. It took thirteen years for the author to create a life out of nothing and find happiness in the end. No journey is easy, but the author reminds us that we need to believe in our vision, have hope to follow through with our dreams, and have the courage to seize them when the moment comes.

Like with the previous section, we end this part with short interactive questions that help the readers engage with what they read and connect their life with the author's experience.

Lastly, section four: 'Paying it Forward - Runway for Hope,' is the fourth pillar of paying it forward, as the title suggests. It is about the creation of the foundation Runway for Hope that the author started in Japan. After decades of moving from one country to another, feeling the displacement of being a refugee, the loneliness of starting a life alone, and wondering all his life how to make the world a better and more colorful place, the author talks about the creation of his organization that was built on giving back.

There were many obstacles that the author faced when creating his own foundation in a foreign country, but the people he met along the way and the team that he built helped make his vision possible. It is with the efforts of many that one small vision could unfold into a unique, impactful foundation. Runway for Hope, the author's foundation, seeks to empower the youth and help those who have faced struggle and hardship in life by bringing awareness through the power of a fashion runway. Since its creation, the program has evolved into so much more.

With dedicated supporters and endorsers, a strong team, and people in need of help, Runway for Hope has created Study Abroad programs that helps underprivileged kids along with a runway show that brings to light the struggle of refugees, displaced peoples, and numerous other people suffering. The organization, which started out small and jumped over various obstacles in the beginning, is now a renowned foundation built on a humanistic mission. With programs such as Runway for Hope's educational platforms, efforts to ease the hardship after the earthquake and tsunami disaster of 2011, and other programs in the work, the author's dream of giving back to the world and mending the gap between the rich and poor has been realized. It is one small step towards a better world, but if we all step together, we can shake the foundation of society and create a better world.

PREFACE
Introducing a Colorful Life

Every day, we live our lives immersed in the haunting truth of reality. Cyber-attacks are growing bigger and stronger, the number of refugees and displaced people are tallying to unbelievable numbers, the militia in various countries have started coups, and thousands of people have died from hunger and poverty. Slowly, the horrible reality of life begins to weigh down on us with impressive force: there was a harassment case at a large firm, war between two impoverished countries, global warming is threatening the livelihoods of displaced animals, children are forced into various labors as slaves -- again and again we are reminded of about the injustice of reality. Whether we are at the mercy of these events or simply a bystander thousands of miles away, there is always something that breaks away humanity little by little.

This leaves us to question: what does it mean to be human if our search for hope, beauty, inspiration, and joy only destroys? What has happened for the world to succumb to such a state? Was it always like this or was there ever a time of bliss and peace?

There comes a time in life when everything is bitter and tasteless; when the color of the sky is no longer blue, and the earth is nowhere close to hues of deep brown and red. In our strange and meaningless life, we look around and try to give meaning to the world around us. There are questions that formulate in our minds, and we begin to reflect on our existence. We don't know why we are or who we are; we don't know where we are heading or where our destination is -- but there is this *feeling* that blooms inside of us, begging us to make sense of it all.

Perhaps there is a simple answer to these questions we ask. Perhaps there will never be an answer to why there is bad in the world or what we can do to make the world a better place. However, despite all the bad that happens in the world and the broken bits of humanity that come crashing down, we are given the gift of *reacting* and *doing*. We don't have to sit around and wait for these problems to be solved by someone else. We have the ability to do something. That is the beauty of it all. "Life is a gift and a journey," as the saying goes, and even if it isn't always as beautiful and as peaceful as we wish, there is no reason to quit and abandon it.

I've learned that no matter what happens or how bad today seems, life goes on. Tomorrow is a new beginning, a time to move forward and take on new challenges. The problems of yesterday are now buried with time, and the bad days we had are nothing but the past.

Life is filled with millions of colors, some of which you cannot see, but exists, nonetheless. Everything in your life gives you color and everyone you interact with shines a light onto the colors you might not have otherwise known existed. Life is as colorful as you make it, it is up to you to allow these colors into your life. Don't just accept the shades of gray that shadow your path but be the ray of a rainbow that lights the darkness.

I've learned that life gives you a second chance and when it does, take it. However, do so in moderation. Accept a helping hand and opportunities when they come around, but don't go through life just by taking what doesn't belong to you. You need to work hard to create things with your own hands. As hard as it is, sometimes you need to be able to let go of your rigid and ingrained beliefs in order to create something out of your life that is truly amazing. Being comfortable and being constrained are two very different things. Know which paths you take are comfortable and which ones constrain you.

In my life, I've learned that if you pursue happiness, it will elude you, but if you focus on what is in front of you and work towards bettering the lives of those who need it, happiness will find you. Furthermore, I've learned that whenever I decide something with an open heart, I usually make the right decision, and that every day, you should reach out and touch someone. As human beings, we need the touch and comfort of another. Holding hands, a warm hug, or just a friendly pat on the back; the act of touch is powerful and can turn a rainy day into a sunny one. Remember that people usually forget what you say, it is what you *do* that they will remember.

Our lives are so much more than what we see on the day-to-day surface. It is easily filled with darkness and more often than not, we forget the joy in life. But life is bigger than we care to realize. Life is more than the house you live in or the building you work in, it is the breeze of the coast of Caspian Sea in Iran; it is watching the whales in northern Canada or feeding the poor on the streets in Pakistan.

Most of us believe that our differences are what make us important and make our lives interesting, but it is when we commonly find beauty that matters the most. Our humanity calls us to search for beauty in the world and look for the beauty within others. Despite our differences, our common humanity is more powerful than our individuality.

That being said, it is usually our differences and our need to clearly stand apart from each other that causes most of the turmoil in the world. We forget that someone with different views is also human. We forget that in another's eyes, *we* are also different. Is it our individuality that matters more, or is it our humanity that will preside over our future? This is the question and the struggle that will define the shape and the soul of this century and next generations to come.

I, myself, was a refugee. I have witnessed what countries and people will do to each other over differences. I've lived through three coup d'etat, faced a Soviet Union invasion, grew up during the Iran and Iraq war, and fled from persecution. I have faced so many hardships over my life, but it was during my childhood when I saw the possibilities of how colorful the world could be. Decade after decade, my life was subjected to struggles in the world that I had no control over. I encountered many problems in life that tried to prevent me from succeeding and moving forward.

I fought through the consequences of wondering *why me?* while trying to build my own future. In spite of it all, I still took the time to walk under the waterfalls of Angels of Venezuela and ventured to Niagara Falls. I grew invested in the education for underprivileged kids in Japan and many other countries all around the world. I bore the passion of helping displaced children from the war in Iraq and Afghanistan. I felt the love of *life* through and through.

The world wasn't just colored in suffering and injustices, but the people I met on my journey through life, the precious moments of beauty and love that I hold close to my heart, those are the colors that really painted the world and my life. No matter where we are in the world or what ailments prevent us from what we want to do, we can all take a moment to love ourselves, our life, and the possibilities of the future.

Know the value of your family and dare to reach out towards the sky. Climb to the top of a mountain and yell at the top of your lungs, "I love you; I thank you for this life, this life of color and of possibilities!" Be grateful for the moments of happiness and remember them in our moments of despair.

It isn't easy to build a life full of color. There will be obstacles, days you feel hopeless, and you lose courage. There will be darkness as well as light, and things are never as they seem or as we expect. We question the world and the things that we don't understand. Use these questions as fuel to a more colorful life. Search for answers, and even if you don't find them, you will find solace in those you encounter along the way.

DISCLAIMER:

This book contains stories and events that the author has gone through and experienced during his lifetime. For privacy reasons, some names in the book have been changed to protect their identity. The photos added in the book may differ + / - 1 year from what is documented.

Although the author had made every effort to ensure that the information in this book was correct at the time of writing and while this publication is designed to provide accurate information in regard to the subject matter covered, the author assume no responsibility for errors, inaccuracies, omissions, images or any other inconsistencies herein and hereby disclaim any liability to any party for any loss, damage, or disruption caused by errors or omissions, whether such errors or omissions result from negligence, accident, or any other cause.

This publication is meant as a source of valuable information for the reader, however it is not meant as a substitute for direct expert assistance. If such a level of assistance is required, the services of a competent professional should be sought.

PART ONE

Dream Big - Start Near

vision

Chapter 1
The Vision of Tomorrow

There comes a time in everyone's life when you begin to question the world around you. Why is the sky blue? Why isn't it pink or purple? Though the questions you ask may vary, it is without a doubt that this time will transpire for the very simple reason: it must. From these simple curiosities come more pressing ponderings that many spend their whole life *not* finding the answers to. Why were we ever born? What is our purpose in life? What happens after we die?

Why ask these questions if we may never find the answer? Why not give up since these questions are beyond our grasp?

The questions that fester inside of us are what gives us life and creates a map to our future. This map is our *vision*. Even if we don't know where the map will take us, we follow it because we want to make our goals and purpose into a reality. Where it leads us and takes us along the way is something we just have to believe is meant to be.

Simply put: Vision is an enlightenment of what it means to be human. It is different from person to person because *we* are all different. Just because we are different doesn't mean one vision is better than the other - they are all unique in their own way and trying to force a certain vision or will it away is futile.

Vision is a force of nature that comes into your life unexpectedly. It comes within and expands without.

Growing up in Iran, I didn't have a particular vision. I was only six and my world was filled with the Baha'i faith that my mother raised me and my brother in. Despite the Islamic thoughts and philosophies that surrounded me in Iran, I was comfortable in my Baha'i household, unphased by the outside world and the dynasty of Iran, which seemed peaceful as far as a six-year-old could tell.

My life didn't have any pressing questions. I believed that the sky was blue because that is what I perceived it to be. Why I was born, my purpose in life, and what happens after death, those questions didn't pose a threat to my peaceful livelihood. Happiness and solace were unbreakable during my life in Iran. Little did I know, however, that life is never as it seems. It changes as time goes on and we have to adjust our body and mind to our surroundings. The comfort and safety we have today isn't a promise for tomorrow.

I was six and my brother, Navid, was only a year old when my family moved to Afghanistan. It was June 1975 and my father, a military ranked officer in Iran, was relocated to Afghanistan as a diplomat. I said goodbye to my small, humble house in Iran, and my family moved to a new country that was to be our home for the next few years.

Omid   My brother, Navid

90% of the population in Afghanistan was Sunni Islam while Iran's population was 95% Shia. Though there was a difference, growing up Baha'i and being a six-year-old, the two main Islam sects seemed to be interchangeable. The differences and borders in the world were invisible to me. We were all the same and, as I thought as a Baha'i, there was oneness to humanity.

Iran and Afghanistan were not only neighbors, but close allies. Iran is very rich in minerals and natural resources such as oil and gas, and back then, was a large creditor to Afghanistan. Because of the amicable relationship between the two countries, Iranian diplomats were welcomed and treated exceptionally in Afghanistan. The house that was provided to us seemed like a castle to me. We had four maids, a chef, gardener, a 24-hour caregiver to watch over me and my brother, along with a guard stationed outside. We were given private cars and a driver who took me to and from school every day. Life in Afghanistan had started out as a dream and even more, we had two new dogs to call our own.

But being six-years old, I wasn't aware of the world, I was only aware of the life that was in front of me. My views in life were as small as I was. I didn't realize how much could change and how much this change was affected by the world around me. The simplest happening or the largest disruption has the ability to rewrite the course of someone's future. Like a stone being thrown into a lake, every ripple has the chance to change the surface of the water.

Moving to the capital city of Afghanistan, Kabul, was the ripple in my life that sparked a change that created *vision* within me.

The first ripple in my life was my first day at an Afghan school. As a six-year-old, I was confused when I first walked in the classroom and saw everyone sitting on the floor in neat lines. The class was already in session and there was no time for introductions. Heeding the rest of the class, I followed suit and took a seat among the other students. I crossed one leg and bent the other. Being in a new environment and surrounded by a new culture was difficult to understand at a young age. I began to notice the differences between cultures and traditions, though I couldn't comprehend what these differences meant.

One of the kids in the class had a book open. The Quran. Since Iran was also a Muslim state, I had heard of the Quran, but growing up in a different faith, Quran was something I never had the chance to truly understand. I was a wide-eyed child in a class full of people who seemed so different from me. It was not easy for me to assimilate and understand their culture and their beliefs. I didn't even understand what the word '*different*' meant.

Students rocked back and forth as someone read from the Quran. Was I supposed to do the same thing? What was the meaning of the movement the other students were doing? Questions filled my head, but instead of trying to find answers to them or think from a bigger perspective, I did what any six-year-old would do and mimicked the rest of the class playfully.

My actions seemed innocent to me. I didn't know what was happening in the class. I didn't know what they were doing, and I didn't know what I was doing. I was simply having fun pretending I was a part of the culture I knew nothing about. However, the teacher quickly took note of my ignorance and my mocking gestures. I was being disrespectful and even though I was new, my behavior was unforgivable.

My teacher yelled at me in front of the whole class, reprimanding my childish behavior harshly before exiling me from the classroom. He followed me out only to scold me more. He told me everything I was doing wrong, but I didn't understand a word he was saying. I cried, not grasping why my actions warranted such anger from the teacher. No one had told me what was happening. My classmates didn't know who I was or why I was there. I felt alone and ashamed.

After the teacher had given me a good scolding, I went back to the classroom, my eyes red and puffy from crying. I wanted to go home. The world seemed to be upside down and I couldn't figure out why it was so hard for me to fit in with the other students. I thought that the worst part of the day was over. Surely, the day couldn't get any worse.

Later during class, I asked the teacher if I could use the restroom. To my dismay, the teacher had said no, and I ended up soiling my pants. I was even more embarrassed than I was during the Quran class and now I had to sit in my soiled pants for the rest of the day.

By the end of the school day, I was crushed. Despite the comfortable life I had back home, everything I did *here* was wrong. When I arrived home, I had told my parents about the awful day I had at school. Being the first son of a diplomat in Afghanistan, my dad was offended by the way I was treated. He had mustered up his innate authority and headed over to the school that evening to give the principal an earful.

I will never forget seeing my father in his military uniform as he took me back to the school to stand up for me. I had seen him many times with it back in Iran, but this was the first time I felt the power he commanded in the uniform. It was at that moment that I knew I wanted to be someone as dynamic as my father. He knew how to work a room; he had charisma, influence, and he was someone compelling. He was not only striking in his uniform, but exuded power in the way I now longed for. I wanted to have the power to protect others while being as handsome and well dressed as him. Although my father had stood up for me that day, my world was already beginning to change.

That day was the only time I ever attended public school in Afghanistan. Afterwards, my parents, along with other diplomat families came together to think of a more constructive plan for diplomat children to learn. The education system was different from Tehran, the capital of Iran, and there was no private or international school in Kabul.

Mr. Daneshvar, a young medical student from Iran, was hired to teach the diplomat children at the embassy compound. While I enjoyed Mr. Daneshvar as a teacher and his teaching style was something I was more comfortable with, I began to wonder about the world around me and notice things I had never noticed before. Though I was back into the routine of life that I was used to, the world was now different in my eyes.

On weekends and short vacations, my family and I would travel to the small towns and villages outside Kabul. It was amazing to see the beautiful nature Afghanistan had to offer. Beige mountains, gassy fields, winding rivers, the beauty of Afghanistan never ceased to be so breathtaking. It was almost as welcoming as the people we met along the way. The kindness and hospitality of the villagers were overwhelming on our travels.

My parents and younger brother in Kabul, Afghanistan - 1978

While there was still the beauty of nature in Kabul and friendly people, walking the streets of the capital, I began to notice the impending hardship all around me. Poverty was apparent in most places I went. I began to wonder if it had always been there. Walking in the market, I'd come across kids, sometimes their guardians, who would approach us and ask for money or other kinds of help. Dirt stained the clothes and streaked the faces of the kids. Their lives and my life were like night and day. There were stark differences that I began to notice between me and other children my age.

45

I was too young to understand the history and politics of the region, yet the gap between the rich and poor didn't go unnoticed. It seemed impossible that there should be such a steep gap. I wanted to know why: What was the difference between us? How can there be such a disparity in society? The problem seemed so blatant that I was sure that the answer to the problem couldn't be so far away. Why were there so many poor people and why wasn't there more stability? Wasn't there any room for them to live a more decent life? What was preventing them from doing so?

Questions about the poverty and hardships I saw after moving to Afghanistan began to flood my thoughts. Every day I wondered what kind of world we lived in and how we got to the point that hardship was a normal part of life. I didn't understand what all of these questions and revelations meant, I only knew that I wanted to become someone who can make a change and lead a movement to solve these problems.

Despite not knowing or understanding the situation going on in Afghanistan, my life and my vision was affected by the history and politics of the country. Although it wasn't apparent when we first moved into our luxurious life as a diplomatic family, the years following had proven to shape me.

In the early 18th century, King Ahmed Shah Durrani unified the Afghan tribes and founded the last Afghan Empire. In 1973, the last king of Afghanistan, Zahir Shah's regime was overthrown by his cousin and former Prime Minister, Daoud Khan. Daoud Khan established a republic and stood as President of Afghanistan until early 1978. Even so, Afghanistan remained in a peaceful state.

It wasn't until the violent coup or "revolution" that had ousted Daoud Khan and created a communist republic that the peace was disturbed. Muhammad Taraki was the leader of the communist republic starting in 1978. This event was followed by two other bloody coups, Hafizulla Amin in early 1979 and then by the Soviet invasion in late 1979. During the later invasion, President Amin was killed, and Babrak Karmal replaced him. There were three Coup d'états, and Soviet Union occupation in a time span that was less than 16 months.

My brother and I on top of a Soviet Union tank
(a few days after 1979 Coup d'état)

These changes that went on within a short period of time had impacted and instilled the importance of vision within me. My questions about the world grew as I got older and had shone a bright light on the differences in the world and the borders that existed. When the political situation in Afghanistan changed, my fear started to grow as well.

The latter years of my life in Afghanistan were painted in colors of fighter airplanes streaking the sky every day and night, the bombardment of certain points in the capital, and tanks or other heavy war machinery in the streets of Kabul. The coup was intent on replacing the government by killing and destroying the capital. It was a dangerous time, and my father taped the windows so that the pressure from a fighter plane flying by wouldn't shatter them.

Though I was 8 when the political situation in Afghanistan began to shift, I still didn't understand how our differences as people could create such violence and chaos. Why were these things happening? What has the world come to? What was so important that a city and its civilians were caught in the crossfire?

Despite the fear that encroached on my life, there were small moments of enlightenment that lit the darkness like a firework against the night sky. My world was caught in the excitement of facing my reality and realizing that life is short and simple. We are given tools and opportunities to conquer and build our future. Despite the hardship and turmoil, I was lucky to live and breathe. Not everyone was as lucky, as I later found out.

Each coup only lasted for a few days, but in those long days, we waited anxiously inside the house. We weren't able to go outside during the coups and we feared every day that the bombs might miss and land on our home. It was terrifying, but when we were finally able to go outside and breathe fresh air, I felt what it meant to be alive and, in that moment, I knew how lucky I was.

Walking the markets after the coups was like walking through a ghost town. The aftermath of a few days was shocking. It wasn't uncommon for the people you see daily on your normal route to be missing. One day they would be in the market selling their wares, and days after the coup, they were no longer there.

I learned to cherish my life and the life of those around me. Even so, the importance of life gnawed at me. What is the importance of life if there are people suffering and living so wretchedly while others live in a comfortable routine? What is the importance of life if there are people trying their best to survive, but are caught in the crossfire of two warring groups? I began to sense that life should have a larger and stronger meaning. It isn't just black and white -- it couldn't be. I wanted to uncover the colors of life and see all that it had to offer.

This was the beginning of change in my life. My time in Afghanistan had forever changed my view of the world. The questions I began asking myself, the importance of life, the vision I was slowly creating in order to reach for these questions and answer them; my small world unfolded into a thousand possibilities.

I began to wonder what kind of world we live in. Why do I study the faith and diversity of humankind if we oppress ourselves and each other? What is humankind trying to achieve by studying faith? What is faith supposed to guide people to? What is the underlying purpose of it all? A door inside my six-year-old mind unlocked. Why are we here? Where are we headed? What is the purpose?

As I got older, I began thinking more about the planet itself. Why is there such destruction and disaster in the world? Why is poverty and hardship never ending? How have human beings been influenced by history and thoughts from thousands of years ago? How has faith and religion been used by society and abused by some leaders and how has it been accepted by people?

What is humanity *truly* trying to achieve? What does it mean to be human?

It only took one day at public school and a walk down a street in Afghanistan to open up my world. A plethora of questions I never knew existed within me blossomed and my whole world was changed. My reality painted itself in different colors and my thoughts about the world, who I was, what faith was to me, had created vivid doors to my future. I started noticing the world more.

I would look up at the night sky and soak up the vastness of it all. The pale sphere of the moon, the impossibility of sunlight reflecting off the surface of the moon and shedding a soft glow onto the planet it orbits around. Why is it that the darkest nights have the brightest stars? How is it that the color of the ocean is a reflection of the sky? Why are rain clouds gray and rain clear?

We are so tiny in this vast universe. There are thousands of small miracles happening every day. The impossibility of life seems endless, but what do I want to do to make an impact? What can I do with my life to give it purpose?

My vision sprung from these questions that began to snowball throughout my childhood. I began to wonder: Can I be a voice within the world that leads others to realize that they are much greater than they think they are? My vision began taking form and I realized the goals in life I wanted to have.

Vision is not something you can just wait for. It is not something you can force yourself to receive either. Vision comes within and expands without.

Vision has everything to do with where you live, what you are surrounded by, and the way you live life. Vision for me is different from your own vision. The questions that lead you to create your vision might contradict my own. They might be controversial and question the society you live in. Whatever questions breathe life into your vision, just know: your vision is your own, built and strengthened by your surroundings and your environment.

It is an enlightenment that each human being is entitled to. A power and an energy that runs through us, all we need to do is develop and nurture it. Think of vision as an ability that we need to practice or a muscle we need to strengthen; alone, our progress is slow and painful, but with help, it is stronger. Our aspirations for the future can't be attained solely by hard work, it is *how* we put in the hard work that matters. It isn't how *fast* we achieve our goals; it is *how* we achieve our goals quickly.

We need to learn and build a *Vision of Tomorrow* because tomorrow is never a promise. There will be many obstacles and struggles you'll face on your path towards vision. As long as we stay curious about the world and question things we don't understand, we will be able to make our future colorful and bright. If you can dream up a vision today, then that gives tomorrow something to fight for.

The Vision of Tomorrow

Chapter 2
Directors in our Lives

Our lives are like a movie. We need a script to follow, actors to bring the script to life, and a director to make sure the vision we see in our script comes out accurately. What comes first is our *vision* or our script. The script, however, cannot *wow* an audience on its own. Without actors willing to breathe life into the script, it is nothing more than a piece of paper and some words. *You* are the actor, and your script is your *vision*. However, it is *how* the movie is directed that dictates if it will succeed in public or not. In the case of life, the director isn't just one person, but the people who surround you and those you look up to. Your parents, your teachers, friends and role models, all of these people play an important role in *how* your *vision* will play out.

There are three key directors in your life: a) *your parents/parental figures*, b) *your teachers and mentors,* and lastly, c) *your friends and peers*. Either intentionally or unintentionally, these people play a large role in making your dreams into a reality. They help you shape and understand your vision so that you may act out your script without hesitation and failure.

After moving to Afghanistan where my world opened up and vision poured out, I turned to my parents for guidance. I didn't ask them or reveal the many questions I had about life, I simply watched how they conducted themselves in life. I lived life beside them and accepted all they had to teach and give me.

I was gifted with a loving and caring mother who, above all, showered me and my siblings with so much affection. She colored my life with the most important touches: tolerance, caring, beauty, love, and so many more that have been instilled within me. She raised me and kept my spiritual sense intact. She filled our household with faith and taught me the importance of keeping it. Though I began to question the meaning of faith, society, and the world, my mother helped guide me to a way of living where I had the ability to make a difference in the world. She is the reason I learned how to appreciate life and support others.

Although my childhood was filled with questions about poverty and the gap of hardship, my mother was the one who gave me courage to follow my vision despite everything happening around me. I questioned the validity of life and its importance as Afghanistan underwent violence and turmoil, but it was my mother's reassurance that comforted my questions and led me to believe that change could happen. She was full of life and resilience, and she taught me to never yield in the darkness.

Mother   Mother and Father - 1976/77

My father was just as important in shaping my vision as my mother was. He was always well dressed and held a silver tongue. I looked up to his authority and charm. How he loved and protected our family was something I had always aspired to. He fed me knowledge, giving me books at a young age. He nourished my curiosity by imparting writing of Leo Tolstoy, Jules Verne, Victor Hugo and stories of Tom Sawyer, Marco Polo, and Tintin - great adventurers who seized the day and sought to uncover their own vision by embarking on adventures and discovering them with their own two hands.

My father, one of the leading directors in my life, was a hero to me. In the times when I was weak and scared, he showed me what it meant to be strong while honing individuality and respect. He showed me how to be disciplined, but not so much that my world was consumed by it. He taught me how to look beyond the horizon, to protect myself while also looking for opportunities to better myself and my life.

These values and principles provided me with a lasting vision and a brighter path in life. The boundless affection and love my parents gave me was the reason I was able to confidently build a future for myself despite all the questions and turmoil that entered my life. My parents were the ones who helped me to believe in myself and my vision and as I got older, I was able to deepen my determination in my professional career and go forward with my life, holding my dreams close.

While my parents were an integral part in creating my script, your life might be swayed by different directors. Everyone's script is unique to their own situation and the directors in your life are similarly unique and tied to the relationships you have. Not all of us are so lucky to be gifted with two parents who support us and give us love. Furthermore, love and support may also look different in different households. The true question isn't how my directors look like your directors; it is *how* the directors in your life nourish your vision. Parental figures aren't the only key directors that support one's vision, there are also peers and friends.

I was sixteen when I was separated from my family. In 1985, during the Iran and Iraq war, I fled from persecution, leaving my family behind. Being alone in the world without knowing when you will ever see your family again is crushing. I was scared, young, and alone in the refugee camp, wondering if I would ever see my parents and siblings again. I wondered every day if I would ever leave the camp and start a new life elsewhere.

It was during this time when friends and peers became an important part in shaping my vision. After years of questioning the world and dealing with hardship myself, I suddenly didn't have my family to turn to for comfort. During my time as a refugee, it wasn't my family who picked me up and directed me to a clearer and stronger vision, it was my friends.

For two years, I lived in Pakistan as a refugee. Though the beginning of my stay was uncertain and difficult, I soon made many friends who shared my pain and suffering. They supported me and breathed life into my future. Due to the situation, we were in, not all of my peers stayed in my lifelong term, but they all had a huge impact on how I saw and viewed the world.

At the refugee camp, my friends became a second family to me and played a considerable role in my life that shaped me to who I am today. I am indebted to them more than they could possibly know. So much of my learning, thoughts, values, career-choices, education, and professionalism is because of the guidance of my friends. If not for them, I wouldn't be the man I am now.

Youth is a malleable time where the things we learn and the company we keep is important to shape our future. Even so, friends are important in all stages of your life. They are the family you choose and not the one you are born into. While parents are the guiding directors in turning your script into a reality, friends are the driving force of your movie taking shape. Friends challenge your vision and your script; they support you and dare you to dream bigger.

Much like friends who impart their own knowledge onto you, teachers and mentors are also another major director in your life. They are the ones who directly open up paths to your future. They inspire your vision to grow and become attainable. We respect the teachers and mentors in our lives because they give our vision hope.

Teachers color your life from early-education to higher-education, extra-curricular schooling to passion hobbies and training coaches, from seniors in your workplace to mentors you respect. All of these role models affect your life differently, but it is without a doubt that they all impart some sort of wisdom onto you. Whether you accept the knowledge they give you is up to you but,

The mentors and teachers that really impact your life are the teachings that embed themselves into your mind and give you strength to continue forward.

There were many people I looked up to when I was growing up. Mr. Daneshvar was one of the earliest directors in my life. He was my teacher who had come to Afghanistan after the incident of attending public school. My philosophy teacher in high school was another mentor I had learned so much from. The third most memorable one was my university professor who taught technology versus the world of spiritualism. All of these teachers had provided me with guidance, bestowing upon me a new way of thinking about the world and people within the world.

Although Mr. Daneshvar entered my life at a very early age, he is a teacher that I will never forget. He taught us an array of knowledge, from basic language to math to many other subjects that were integral parts of primary school. I respected him very much. He was a very caring gentleman who was always well-spoken and a teacher who impacted my life from a young age. Aside from teaching us basic knowledge, he encouraged us to be strong and helped us along the way.

During the rollercoaster life many of us had while living in Kabul at the time, he was the solid rock that kept us grounded outside of home life. He connected with us by sharing his life stories and the hardships he had gone through at a young age. He gave us courage to fight for our dreams by sharing how he fought for his dreams during times of hardships.

However, it wasn't just my teachers who I saw as my mentors and role models, but the various stories I was exposed to. My father provided me with novels that were meant for readers beyond my age, but I devoured these stories. The knowledge I found in books encouraged me and made me believe that I could achieve greatness.

Directors in our Lives

As a boy living throughout Afghanistan, India, Pakistan, and Iran during a time of hardship, turmoil, and bloodshed, I was lucky enough to live on the more luxurious side of life. I was fascinated with the odysseys of TinTin along with the extraordinary lives of Gandhi and Marco Polo, all of whom had inspired me to achieve the vision I had created. The epic life and poems by Ferdowsi, Rumi (Molana), Saaddi also played a factor in shaping my life and driving me to dream big, brighter, and more colorful.

I was inspired by all of these role models, great thinkers, explorers, and fictional characters that became *directors* in my journey to achieving my vision. Though I didn't know them personally and they didn't teach me in the traditional sense, there was an abundance of value I took away from their stories and lives.

Teachers and mentors come in all different times, shapes, sizes, and modes. In a more modern sense, children nowadays look up to characters existing in the animated world. From superpowers and saviors in the world of Popeye and Superman, there are many fictional role models that children have the opportunity to be influenced by. Harry Potter, Wonder Woman, Disney characters, and so on have the potential to be great educational aids to children in need of important directors in their life.

Not everyone is blessed with a good family and strong friendships. Despite these characters and stories being fictional, it is important that children have *directors* in their lives to help support the dream and vision they are trying to nurture.

Having vision isn't always easy. Whatever made you question the world and help you create your *vision* may have come from rocky transitions, horrible experiences, confusing transformations, and other negative situations during childhood.

However, it is the nourishment and support we get from the directors in our lives (family, friends, mentors, role models) that allow us to believe in ourselves.

The people who surround you with affection, give you support, and comfort are the kings and queens in your life; the true heroes that help you achieve your happy ending. Amidst all the turmoil in the world, they are the ones who will welcome you with open arms and offer their love no matter what happens.

Vision cannot be achieved alone. Just as a flower needs nutrition from the sun and the rain, we also need others to make us strong and raise us up. Without good directors to help the actor and support the script, the chances of falling and failing are high. Not everyone in your life can be a good director and the bad ones we come across only make us realize how lucky we are when we find someone who is willing to support us in our endeavors.

Do you remember the first time someone made fun of your dreams? When was it that you started feeling that your dreams were insignificant or that you would never be able to achieve them? Were those your thoughts or the thoughts of those around you?

Self-doubt isn't uncommon, especially as you grow into an adult or go through big transitions in your life. Every day, there are forces that work against you to make you question the validity of your resolve. Sometimes these factors are the bad directors in your life telling you that you can't succeed. However, their questions and negativity toward your dreams *aren't* because they don't believe in your ability to make something of yourself, it is their own lack of self-confidence and their fear of what you *could* achieve that makes them target you and feed you with negative thoughts.

These people in your life feed off of your misery and self-deprecation that they instill in you. They believe that if you are small, then it gives them a better chance to succeed with their own vision in life. But vision isn't something you can accomplish alone nor is it something you can accomplish by hindering others who are trying to achieve their goals. Whenever someone puts you down and makes you second guess the validity of your script, keep a clear head and remember that you are the master of your own life.

You are the creator of your own script. *You* are the actor who will bring your script to life. *You* get to decide who are the directors in your life. Will you listen to the bad directors who feed you negativity or will you stand by those who hold you up when you are down?

As a child, you come across many people who are older and *seem* wiser than you. These adults will advise you and try to feed you their own wisdom. It is inevitable that you'll accept these words and hold onto them as truth. Whether it is because of the pressure we feel from our parents or by tradition, we take these words with respect, not questioning the knowledge you've gained.

On the other hand, you'll come across peers your own age, who will either belittle your dreams or give you courage to continue forward. Whether it is discouragement or encouragement you receive, sometimes it feels as if the negativity outweighs the positivity. However, instead of being burdened by negative thoughts, turn them into a source of light that will give you an advantage. Let those who will always be negative towards your goals be negative. If they put you down, never believe in you, or make fun of you, let them. Your dreams are too valuable to let insecure people sway your determination.

Don't waste valuable time wondering why they think the way they do or how to remedy their thoughts of you. You already know what they have to say to you, so don't try to understand *why* they say the things they do. The key isn't finding who they are and what they want from you. The key is to discover who you truly are, and their hurtful words will just tear down your confidence in that.

Take their words as pearls of wisdom. Use every single negative comment to build your strength and set yourself more firmly on your path.

It is imperative to have negative thoughts and comments in your life because with them you can create a vision more constructively and find the will to make it happen. Despite directors in your life being your source of nourishment, you, as an individual, have to be strong and listen to the direction of those who speak to you out of a place of love and support. It can be hard sometimes because self-doubt is a strong force that makes our vision waiver. Whenever we waiver, the voices of our bad directors come back to us, coaxing us into submission.

Just remember self-doubt is the critics that rate our movie as a failure before it is even released.

Directors of the *World Within* and the *World Without*

Focus on yourself and what you can do with what you are given. What can you do with the hateful words? What can you do with the questions you ask and the vision you create? How can you utilize the knowledge gained from the directors in your life? Our dreams we have of tomorrow are built inside of us. It is something not yet tangible and even so, we can see how our future would unfold if life played out perfectly. We spend years reaching for this dream in attempts to materialize it before the world *within* creates the world *without*.

The directors in our lives are the ones to support our vision. They give us opportunities to bring our dreams into the *world without*. However, before we can formulate our vision into something tangible, it is imperative that we first understand the world within: our dreams and vision. Once we understand the world within, we can use it to maneuver the world without.

If you think about all the people who have changed the world, for better or for worse, they all understood the world within and used it to control the world without. *"I don't live by all these weird, rigid rules that make me feel fenced in. I just like the way that I feel, and that makes me very free."* Adolf Hitler isn't a man that many people want to be like. The destruction and hurt he brought into the world have been scorched into history forever, yet his vision was one that came within and expanded without.

The world within is our cause and the world without is the effect. The inner always governs the outer, and the outer is a reflection of the inner. Just so, the outer conditions mirror the inner consciousness. These two worlds are not separate, but they are two different levels of the same world.

"*You must not lose faith in humanity. Humanity is an ocean; if a few drops of the ocean are dirty, the ocean doesn't become dirty.*" Gandhi was another man who had changed the world. Though instead of instilling fear like Hitler, he had inspired and brightened the world. His vision was one that came within and expanded without.

Gandhi was a great man who had taken his vision into his own hands and tried to enlighten the vision of others. Unlike the bad directors in life, Gandhi was one of the few whose guidance transcended time and space, still having a pull on the world despite his departure from it.

"*We but mirror the world. All the tendencies present in the outer world are to be found in the world of our body. If we could change ourselves, the tendencies in the world would also change. As a man changes his own nature, so does the attitude of the world change towards him. This is the divine mystery supreme. A wonderful thing it is and the source of our happiness. We need not wait to see what others do.*"

-Mahatma Gandhi

The real change comes when we go within and do the work of inner transformation. To examine ourselves openly, honestly, vulnerably and to purge out any resemblance of selfishness, immorality or insecurity. Only then will we be able to truly understand the world within and control our world without.

Gandhi was pointing to the foundation upon which a lot of today's "spiritual" teachings draw their rationale from. He guided us deeper to do the inner work that we often shy away from; the inner change beyond simply wishing or visualizing.

When you look at his life, even in his weakness and mistakes, he was searching to pardon himself of selfish desires and develop his capacity to be used as an instrument in the service to his fellow beings. The concept of "non-violence" as it is generally interpreted, revolves around the consideration of the welfare of other beings. The more we are consumed with our own affairs, the less room we have for others, for truth, for God or for whoever or whatever we believe in.

Vision is a unique part of everyone's life, sculpted by your surroundings and people who play an integral part of your life. Good or bad, right or wrong, vision is a boundless frontier that comes in many shapes and sizes. It is *what* you do with your vision and *how* you apply the support you've been given from the directors in your life. If the acting in your life's movie is half-hearted, it wouldn't matter that your dreams are momentous or how amazing the encouragement from your directors are; ultimately, it is up to you to paint your life with color. Seize the brush of fate and create every stroke with meaning and intention. You are the master of your will.

Directors in our Lives

Chapter 3
Vision of Change

"Yesterday I was clever, so I wanted to change the world.
Today I am wise, so I am changing myself."
-Jalal Din Mohammad Rumi (Molana)
Persian Poet and philosopher.

Only the wise know that they have to be the change that they want in the world.

Many of us, whether from an early age or later on, tend to believe we have the ability to change the problems and dissatisfaction we witness every day. During my time in Afghanistan, Pakistan and India, I was a kid who dreamed of changing the world.

During our stay in Afghanistan where my father was stationed between 1975 to 1980, we often traveled to other countries, either for vacation or to visit my father who would be away from us for a month or so while he was on duty. There was one country in particular that contributed to my changed view of the world: India.

While often renowned for the Taj Mahal, India is one of the most extraordinary countries on the planet. It is home to one of the oldest civilizations in the world and it is a mosaic of multicultural experiences. The country has a rich heritage along with thousands of religions and beliefs. It is truly a marvelous place to visit.

Mother and younger brother - Taj Mahal, India 1978

However, despite all the wonders India has to offer, I distinctly recall the poverty and large crowds I would see on the streets as a boy. My brother, Navid, and I were very fortunate to visit and learn so much about India, and though we enjoyed playing together while we were there, the poverty I saw was astonishing.

While Afghanistan had its own issues, and the hardship I saw there had struck a new world view within me, it was my visits to India that really inspired my desire to change the world. I was taken aback by how many people were facing hardship and poverty. Afghanistan was considered one of the least developed countries in the world, so the poverty and hardship I found there was to be suspected. But India was bustling with life and culture, the prospects in India were starkly contrasted against the poverty-ridden population that seemed to overflow the streets of the country.

I came across so many kids my age who were begging in the street, knowing nothing but the hard work of just living life each and every day. The abnormality of the situation was incredibly painful for me to witness. Even to this day, decades after my childhood visits, the image of poverty and orphan children facing malnutrition motivates me to do something meaningful in the world.

At that time, I kept asking my parents, *"Why are the poor, poor? Why don't they have anyone to care for them or help them?"* These questions, sprung from my original vision I found in Afghanistan, made me realize how lucky I was to have two parents who loved and cared for me. I was lucky to have a roof over my head and a warm meal to eat.

Baha'i House - Delhi, India 1978

This feeling of wanting to change the world festered within me during my childhood and I sought solutions to fix the problems I saw. Although I was too little to make a big change, I was young enough to learn and soak up the knowledge the world had to offer me. I devoted myself to knowing and *truly* understanding why there was a massive disparity in the world and how it began. Some of the questions I sought to solve had endless answers that were built upon centuries of disparity.

How massive and complicated these problems were and the history behind these problems only led to so many other questions. I spoke to those who suffered. I instilled within myself the feeling of being poor and suffering. My life was a rollercoaster, and I was blessed to see both sides of the world during my youth.

Nonetheless, it was hard to sustain my vision of making a difference because I was just a child. There was only so much I was capable of doing at that time in my life. On top of my limited ability to take action, there were other circumstances such as war, turmoil, revolution, and the lack of stability that got in my way.

Like so many children, I wanted to do something bigger than myself. I *believed* I could change the world. I even thought about building an orphanage to help poor children. My dreams of change were big, yet I was small. Many obstacles that got in the way of my childhood visions and dreams. The revolution in Iran, the Iran and Iraq war, and many other incidences displaced my vision. I wasn't able to follow through the way I had fantasized about. However, failure isn't the end, it is the chance for a new beginning.

Even with all of these other factors that might play against your vision, don't lose focus. Keep faith and build on it.

When you work towards your vision, things won't always go as smoothly as you expect. These bumps in the road aren't there to weaken you and prevent you from moving forward, they are there to strengthen you. They will make you more secure in your path and more cautious in the future.

Create a certain number of visions, don't just let one be the epitome of your life. Nurture as many visions as you can hold onto; follow through and do the best you can to reach them. There is no certainty in life that promises you will reach any of the visions you create -- and that is okay. If you are able to take hold of one of them, then you've succeeded in something others are continuing to strive towards. If, by chance, you are able to attain all of the visions that you have created, you are one of the luckiest people in the world and you should be proud of your efforts and hard work. But failing your vision and not achieving any of them should never be considered a bad or negative thing. Being courageous, determined and striving towards your vision is a huge accomplishment. Failing just means you can start anew.

My life took me from place to place as a child. I went from Iran to Afghanistan, visited Pakistan and India several times, moved back to Iran and ended up in a refugee camp in Pakistan where I stayed until I was able to jump start a new life in Canada. All of these changes in my life affected my dreams and the goals I had. Even though I had visions I loved and wanted to follow through with, time goes on and your priority changes as you get older.

When I was younger, I wanted to be a professional football (soccer) player, but there were so many things that worked against me achieving this vision. My love for football had existed within me since I was an elementary school student. I would see my cousins and my neighborhood friends playing, and I longed to join them. Unfortunately, it was a vision my parents were against. They did not want me to take part in playing football mainly because they worried about health and injuries I would sustain, along with it taking away from my education.

Even though my parents were against this vision, it was still something I was passionate about and a dream I wanted to work towards no matter the cost. So, I would play football whenever I could, hiding the truth from my parents or taking up the opportunity to play during physical education time at school.

I grew envious and angry whenever I would see my peers playing football. I was forbidden from participating and it riled me up to see others playing so freely. These emotions fueled my desire to do something about the situation I was in. Since I could not do what I loved without going against my parents openly, the inner aspiration to become a professional football player developed to extraordinary lengths. I carried around my desires, hoping that one day, I would be able to fulfill my vision I had been nurturing.

In 1985, at the age of sixteen, I was forced to leave my family and flee from Iran to Pakistan. I spent two years as a refugee with thousands of other refugees. Although it was extremely hard to be away from my family and surrounded by people I didn't know, I felt a sort of freedom I never had when I was with my parents. I felt like I was finally free to do whatever I wanted.

Life as a refugee was very difficult, and though I made a lot of friends there, it was still an uncertain time where everyone was anxious to move on from our situation. However, the greatest joy I found during this time in my life was the freedom to play football with other refugees and locals. Most of them were much older than me, and because of the age gap and my lack of experience, there were so many times when they wouldn't allow me to play with them.

Pakistan - Refugee period 1986/87   Tournament organized by refugees 1987

It was hard having a huge passion for something, but not being allowed to be given the chance to hone it. Even during times when I played among friends, I wasn't picked for teams due to my smaller physical stature. It hurts to be left out. I had studied the sport for many years, and I knew that I had the confidence in myself to be better than my peers.

I had to wait another few years before I could further my vision in becoming a semi-professional football player. At the age of seventeen, I was headed out of the refugee camp and into Canada. I was eager to finally apply myself to my dreams when I started my new life. I could play how I wanted with the freedom to play where no one would tell me that I wasn't good enough. I could use the discipline I found within and bring it to my world without.

I had the whole world, my life and my freedom in front of me that was mine to build upon. I had so much hope and my dreams felt tangible. I practiced and studied football as much as I could in a very short period of time. I got chosen to play on the varsity team at my university and then I went on to play for the Montreal League. I was finally taking steps towards the goal I had carefully kept and planned for since I was a child. Playing varsity for my university team was the door that opened up the opportunity I had to play for a higher level and professional league.

I was captain of my university futsal team, and we were champions for 3 years in a row in Montreal, Canada. Furthermore, I was invited to a summer camp for the Canada men's national soccer team, but due to some internal disputes, I was not selected for the final roster. A few years later, after coming out of a long injury recovery, I took another chance at attaining my goal. I had moved to England to complete my doctorate and I was selected to be a part of the first team of my college in Cambridge. I was thirty-one at this time and one of the oldest players on the team. Despite many things working against me, I still strove for my dreams that grew farther and farther away as I got older.

Sidney Sussex College, University of Cambridge 2002

Looking back now, I wish I would have had the encouragement and the push I needed to follow through with my dream from the directors in my life. Without directors to help foster your dreams and encourage you to achieve your goals, it is difficult to attain them. Although I had people supporting me, being a professional football player was one of my biggest dreams and the vision that needed my closest directors. Throughout all my years in Canada and as I moved abroad to further my education, I still hadn't seen my parents. By the time I was in England and selected to be a part of the football team, it had been over ten years since I last saw them. I needed them the most, but because of life events and misfortune, I hadn't gotten the opportunity to reconnect with my family.

Even if you have a big dream and you take opportunities to reach your dream, you need the foundations of your vision. I wish I had the encouragement and right nurturing from the directors in my life. I wish they had seen the passion and desire in me that I knew I had, seen my potential and helped me train. However, lamenting over what could have been will only hold me back. Despite my dreams of being a professional football player failing, I learned so much from my failures and I used it to create new avenues for my future.

Nonetheless, I don't blame my family or friends for the lack of support I received for this vision of mine. They had given me so much in different aspects of my life and because of the environment they lived in, the lack of security, the turmoil and violence going on all around them, they weren't able to nurture all aspects of my vision. My parents did their best to raise their children to be people worthy of making the world a better place. Despite the obstacles in my childhood, they gave us the nurturing that was within their capacity.

On the bright side, having all of these negative words, rejections and doubts from many people around me gave me strength. It gave me the desire to prove them wrong and to be better than what they expected of me or what they could not see. I was able to apply myself to this vision and fully focus on doing something I am passionate about and believe in.

Even though I worked hard and was determined towards this goal, I still failed. What made matters worse is that I failed the *expectations* I had for myself. I could not reach the top as I envisioned and planned and knowing that I had failed had greatly disappointed me. But my disappointment didn't enable dark thoughts to rule over my life. No matter how bitter it was to accept my defeat, I knew that I had to accept my disappointment and I had to find a way to live with it instead of living *under* it.

Failure, disappointment, fear, and uncertainty are all a part of the journey we take through life and by accepting it, we learn to be resilient, resolute and grow into a more diligent and courageous person.

Sometimes there are reasons behind why you fail and why your vision doesn't take shape the way you had planned and hoped that you cannot change. Due to forces of nature, lifestyle, changes within your life, family interference, and many more, your vision isn't something only you have the power over. There are forces in your life that are beyond your control.

Think of a flower. It needs the rain and sun to grow, but just as the rain and sun nurture the flower, they can also be the reason for wearing and tearing the leaves or petals. A heavy rainstorm may damage the exterior of the flower, but it is flexible and will heal with time. Even if the timing of your dream prevents you from achieving it, or there are other forces in your life that damage your vision, you are fearless, flexible and focused.

We can't always plan for the future. It is an ever-changing road that has twists and turns. Those who've directed you in your life may also be the ones who prevent you from your dreams or cause a ripple for great change. You need to be mindful of the changes that could happen and use flexibility as an asset in your dreams and not just the path to take after failure.

Dreams aren't yours to bear alone. While you are the master of your own will and each accomplishment you achieve, there is no single or small achievement in life that you've completed all on your own. There are always other factors and people in your life who have been involved in your dream to help you along the way. The tiniest interaction could be the cause for the biggest change in your life.

Everything we do in life has a reason and a force behind it. It is a natural phenomenon, and no one can deny it. Whether it be a teaching from the past, revenge for something experienced, prejudice that was built throughout time, or a million other forces of consciousness, there is always an outside force stemming from your decisions. A singular action does not exist.

As humans, we are strongly bound to each other and complement one another. There are people who may believe and claim that they did everything themselves and created where they are in life out of *their own* hard work, but that is simply impossible. Without any external or secondary force to gain what you've dreamt of doing, there is nothing. Even the dreams you hold onto were born out of questions you asked about the world around you. These questions then turn into a keen observation about the world that inspired you to do something within life. There are forces acting upon you just as you are acting upon them by creating a vision.

With this in mind, even if you cultivated your vision and ended up failing or not seeing your vision to the end, you should be proud of how far you came. The time you spent studying, planning, changing your life in order to complete your vision, wasn't in vain. Though you've lost something major in your life, remember that you must have gained something out of it. If not knowledge, then an enrichment to life in knowing that.

If life seems bleak and the sky broods with darkness, remember that tomorrow is a different day. The sun will rise again, and the dark skies of yesterday will be nothing but a memory - a lesson for your future. It isn't an ending, but a new chapter in your life. Start again when you have failed. When your vision is lost, rebuild what you've cultivated and turn it into something bigger and better. If you dare to look beyond, you will see a whole new dawn where new opportunities and interests thrive. Never end your vision or quit, just imagine and create a new one. Don't close your book, turn the page to a new chapter.

Chapter 4
Final Destination

Once you begin to build your vision and dream beyond, there are steps you need to take to keep your pace and not lose your concentration.

"For yesterday is but a dream, and tomorrow is only a vision; but today well lived makes every yesterday a dream of happiness, and tomorrow a vision of hope."
- Unknown Author, Ancient Buddhist Literature

You cultivate your dreams by asking questions about the world. Dare to be curious about society, the structure of your life, and the world around you. Don't hold back when it comes to dreaming; the world is what you make of it, and it is yours to understand. Although *you* must create your own vision, it isn't something that you need to work towards alone. There are so many people in your life who will support you and enlighten your path towards vision. Follow those who will direct you towards greatness, not those who work to tear down all the hard work you've put in. Use the doubt you'll encounter as a means to rise higher and achieve greater.

While having vision may seem like a daunting task to achieve, don't run away from the possibilities of your future. There are many people who've dared to dream but didn't have the courage to carry on through the journey. Be the one to path the way to a brighter future for those who will follow. The world will open up to you if you just *try*. 2

Failure might be inevitable but keep flexibility on the horizon and work around the situations you encounter. Don't just nurture one dream, but sow as many visions as your passions allow. Just because one door closes, doesn't mean that there aren't others you can't enter. Use the knowledge you gained by chasing after one dream to be the foundation for a new one.

To dream far and beyond, there are two things that are essential practices to keep in mind. First, you must be focused. Working towards *vision* is a lifelong journey that you need to nurture along the way. Secondly, it is never, *ever* too late to dream big. Don't hold back because you never know what the future may hold.

"I alone cannot change the world, but I can cast a stone across waters to create many ripples."

-Mother Theresa

Life is a stone throw of choices you make and the ripples of impact you have on others throughout your life. As we've said before, everyone has their own vision, their own script that they act to. You are just as valuable as a director in someone else's script as you are an actor to your own script.

Determination, planning, keeping faith, and taking action are important factors to keep in mind when guiding your own vision and creating your future.

DETERMINATION

Determination is a massive key to achieving your goals. Be determined in your dreams so that one day they become your reality. In other words, whatever you dream, be it big or small, make sure you are determined to give everything you have to make it come true. Otherwise, your dream won't get you anywhere. It will simply be a burdensome thought you'll have to carry around with you.

Your *passion* and *hunger* are the principles to your success in achieving your dreams. They are what will keep the fire burning within you and allow you to not lose focus. Those who do not give up no matter the pressure they are facing are the ones who will have the advantage of a stronger mind and a will of steel. Even if you have unwavering determination and aren't able to reach your goal, you will undoubtedly attain a future that shows your level of mental strength.

Each human is gifted with something, be it art, sports, intellect, strength, perseverance, etc. However, unlocking the potential that lingers within all of us depends on how we grasp and utilize the special talent within and bring it without. There will always be opportunities that come to your doorstep. If you are not passionate enough with your vision, the possibility of missing the opportunity is great.

Though your failure towards your vision doesn't hinge solely upon the opportunities that greet you, they are a pivotal point in achieving your dreams. You never know what opportunity will be the foot in the door that you need to delve further into your vision. Without the proper determination, the work that goes into your vision could be more difficult or time consuming. Being prepared for opportunities and having the courage to go forth and grab them might be the biggest difference between failure and success.

PLAN

While determination is important, it isn't enough to guide your vision to success. It is always a good idea to have a plan, and a good one at that. However, it is important to note that this step varies from vision to vision, and from person to person.

A "good plan" for me may be different from your good plan. Just as your vision is dependent on the environment you grow up in, the family you have, the people you surround yourself with and the mentality of your society and culture, your plan is also affected by the same thing.

A person born and raised in the Middle East and Africa will see planning differently than someone from Germany or Japan. People who have grown up bearing the weight of hardship and witnessing bloodshed may be more concerned about how to live each day rather than planning for the future. They may plan in a less systematic and traditional way, but they are still able to achieve their goals, ending up with success and high results.

In fact, throughout the last century, there have been many people who have been globally recognized that have achieved big dreams who have come from places where hardship was inevitable or have experienced the unfairness of life at some point in their life. Rather than those going through well-organized communities and thriving with all life has to offer, these people stood out against the crowd and fought for their dreams with everything they had.

A person who grew up in comfort and had access to luxuries in life where they received full support from their guardians and peers would likely plan in a different, more structured way. The thoughts of *Will I live tomorrow?* or *How much will I have to risk achieving my dreams?* may not cross the mind of someone who lives a life of comfort and safety.

When you have not been through the life of a Palestinian father, an Afghan mother or a Syrian kid who, since their birth, have struggled and never seen a day of peace and normal life, you will not understand the day-to-day planning of trying to stay alive. The way these people plan and move forward in life is distinctively different from those living in industrial and developed countries. Even though many of these people have not received a straightforward education, they have great vision that isn't measurable by their simple plan. It is their eagerness and their perseverance of their past that makes them strong and their will impenetrable.

Nevertheless, there is no perfect plan. Whether you are from a life of comfort or one of hardship, follow your natural instincts, your confidence, and let your determination be the driving force behind your vision. There are millions of successful and well accomplished people on this planet who have been raised in less-than-ideal environments. No matter where you are in life, you are not alone. Just because your plan may look different from another doesn't mean the value of your chance for success is different.

KEEPING FAITH

"Made weak by time and fate, but strong in will
To strive, to seek, to find, and not to yield."

- Ulysses poem by Alfred Lord Tennyson

By keeping faith in your determination and your plan, moving forward towards your goal will be easier. Don't lose hope nor give up. There will come times when you fall down and recovering from the fall may be hard, but it is a part of your journey to your vision. Even if your plans are not what you had hoped for or your surroundings unexpectedly fail you, there is hope in the future.

Your world won't end just because your plan failed. Sometimes you have to let go and begin in a new chapter with more enthusiasm and determination. There is more to life than just what we might see today.

Don't be afraid to rise up above your expectations and believe in your instincts. Trust that you are not alone and remember that not every rainstorm births a rainbow, but after every rainstorm breaks a blue sky.

The more you fall, the better you will become. Learn from your failures and don't lose faith over obstacles that try to set you back. With practice, you will become stronger both mentally and physically. If vision was easy to achieve, everyone would live happily and be successful in their own respect. Trust the process and know that after a rainy day, the sun will shine.

ACTION

It is the action you take when faced with darkness that brings your vision to life.

For an *Artist*, dreams are what you imagine beyond creating a work of art. To a *Chef*, dreams stem in your taste buds, longing to create a recipe that will transport the consumer to a different world. Perhaps, to an *Engineer*, dreams are defined by building a machine unlike anything anyone has seen. An *Astrophysicist* would dream of going beyond our planet to find life somewhere else in the universe. Unbounded creativity is key to unlocking our visions, all we have to do is seize it for ourselves.

Not everyone can become a great Artist, but great artists can come from anywhere.

Action is highly vital to the success of your vision because it completes your path and the journey you traveled throughout your life. Without action, everything else is useless and there is no point in continuing on. As such, your vision for your future has become nothing more than a failure without a new beginning. No matter how hard it is to move forward, taking action is a necessary part of your vision.

Each of us has a unique dream, but building our vision is a common goal shared among all of us. When we are able to hold onto our vision, plan for it, keep our determination and not lose faith, crossing over the bridge of success is like a breath of fresh air. You are born into someone who has achieved and worked hard to create something out of a mere dream.

Take action and not let worries affect the path you are on. It is wise to be cautious but foolish to let the fear immobilize you on your journey. No matter how determined you are, how much you plan, or how desperately you hold onto your vision, nothing will happen if you don't take action. Nurture the world within that allows your dreams and your vision to flourish, but don't neglect the world without.

Any step towards your vision is a risk. Depending on your situation, it could be a risk just to *have* a vision and a dream. Everyone's experience is different and the action each person has to take to fulfill their dreams varies, but it is without a doubt that *action* is the determined plan you take toward your vision, with full faith that you will and *can* succeed.

No matter your situation. No matter how different your vision or plan may look compared to others. No matter how bleak the world is or how many voices tell you that you can't. No matter what, success is possible. It is possible despite it all. All you have to do is act.

Take the iconic football player, Pele, as an example of action and vision well panned out.

Pele was called the "King of Football" during his active years, though his beginnings were anything but. He was a legendary sports figure that many looked up to, not just because of his amazing football skills, but because of what he meant for people who shared his background and his journey.

Struck and raised in poverty, Pele's childhood was tied to various odd jobs, anything to earn extra money. In his early days, he could not even afford buying a proper football, but that didn't stop him from chasing after his dreams. He would take socks and stuff them with newspaper, tied with a string or grapefruit.

A major director in Pele's life was his father who had taught him to play football. Pele then went on to play for various amateur teams in his youth. His beginnings were humble if not defined by poverty and a life of hardship. His dreams were large, but so was his determination. Not everyone is so lucky to achieve their dreams to the scale that Pele has, but he is the light in a dark tunnel. He is an aspiration of hope.

Pele's determination and hard work had opened up many opportunities for him. He joined the Brazil national team and helped them win the World Cup in 1958, 1962, and 1970 -- a record among so many others that no one else has ever reached, to this date. Among many awards and honorary nominations, he was appointed as a UN ambassador for the environment in 1992, UNESCO Goodwill Ambassador in 1995, and Football Player and 'Athlete of the Century' by the International Olympic Committee in 1999.

The renowned football player had taken his dreams and not only fulfilled them, but he reached for the stars and came away with stardust. His extraordinary life of success couldn't have been easy for Pele. There are risks in every decision you make as you work towards your goal. Sometimes these risks aren't worth the consequences, but other times they pay off in more ways than you can imagine.

Not everyone will be able to achieve their dreams. No matter how hard you work towards them, there will always be a chance of failure, which is just the hard fact of life. However, the future is unpredictable and what might be false today could be true tomorrow. Don't regret not taking action because you are scared. It is better to try and fail than to not have tried at all.

It doesn't matter where you come from, how brutal or gentle your life is or isn't. If you build a vision and you are fully determined, ready to fight for your future without losing hope, you will reach the horizon and achieve things in your life you never imagined of achieving.

Having vision in life makes your life more colorful. It shades it with opportunities of hope and dreams, coloring the empty parts of your life with colors beyond your imagination. The world holds an endless number of colors and having vision is just one way to turn the gray tones of an uncertain life into something with meaning and purpose.

Vision adds color to your life, but the importance of life focuses on the reality of where we are born, how we live, and in what state we leave this world. These are the most important factors to our existence and well-being. To be remembered as a worthy human being while paying it forward and being an overall *good* person. More than anything, don't forget who you are and those directors in your life who have contributed to the path you took. Consider them as treasures in life and every hiccup you make on your way, a valuable lesson.

Reflection Activity

■ Write down the Key Points you took away from Part One?

_____

_____

_____

_____

_____

_____

_____

_____

_____

_____

_____

_____

_____

_____

_____

_____

_____

_____

_____

_____

1. What are my Dreams?

_____

_____

_____

_____

_____

_____

_____

_____

_____

2. What can I do to build my dreams, so they are something worth
   fighting for?

_____

_____

_____

_____

_____

_____

_____

_____

3. Who are the key directors in my life?

_____

_____

_____

_____

_____

_____

_____

_____

4. What and Who are the figures downplaying my dream/vision? How should I implement their comments so that it empowers my dreams rather than take away from them?

_____

_____

_____

_____

_____

_____

_____

_____

_____

5. How will you stay determined in your dream?

_____

_____

_____

_____

_____

_____

_____

_____

6. What is one thing you've planned for your vision?

_____

_____

_____

_____

_____
_____
_____
_____
_____

7. What will you do if you lose faith in your dream? What is your
   silver lining?

_____
_____
_____
_____
_____
_____
_____
_____

8. How can we build our dreams and then put them to action?

_____
_____
_____
_____
_____
_____
_____
_____

Vision comes within and expands without - coloring your life through and through! Dare to ask questions about the world around you, live in the moments of your success, and don't be afraid of failure. Your life is what you make it; do what you can today because yesterday's efforts are the building blocks of tomorrow.

PART TWO

Value Yourself - Appreciate Loved Ones

hope

Chapter 1
The Value of Life - Live in it, Don't Lose it

The vibrancy of the world is like a rainbow after a storm, or a flower garden that reaches out towards the horizon. Each nation contributes a different color to the overall beauty that is. Tribes, religions, races, languages, traditions, cultures, these are only a part of what makes life more beautiful. The differences that exist in the world, which change when you cross borders or oceans, are what paints the world in an array of colors.

What would happen if the world was nothing more than black or white? Would a rainbow still be beautiful if it was only one color? What if a flower garden birthed nothing but weeds - would it still hold the same transformative awe?

We are what colors life and the world around us. Everything we touch, everything we *do* plays a part in making the world into a rainbow or a flower garden. We are all the colors of life, and we live together in harmony to make this world more beautiful. Just as we have directors in life that guide our *vision*, we are the colors that inspire *hope* to those around us, and vice versa, the colors that others harbor within give *us* the hope we need to move forward.

"Hope is being able to see that there is light despite all of the darkness."

- Desmond Tutu

Each human being is the light others find at the end of a dark tunnel. We can never know for certain how many people we have helped and touched on our journey in life. There are people who may be thankful to you just for your presence. You could bring the brightness to their lives just by being who you are today. Maybe you haven't realized it yet, but it is there.

Life shouldn't just be living *through* the motions of the day and looking forward to the weekend to come. Life should excite and inspire every day. Be grateful for each moment you are alive and hold onto the time you have, reminding yourself of those who aren't in your life anymore. Remember those who have left you with lingering regret about something you said or something you should have done. Think often about the people in your life you miss dearly, and wish could be beside you, watching you grow, witnessing your achievements, and comforting your pain and sorrow. Remember the love you shared and moments you've spent with these people who've helped bring color to your life.

I vividly recall the first time I felt the importance of life. How fleeting and short it could be. I was only 8 years old.

My childhood wasn't the easiest, and though there were moments of luxury and bliss, the world around me darkened as I got older. During the first coup d'état, I didn't understand what was happening. The planes streaking overhead and the volume that the world erupted in was all overwhelming. In a few days' time, I realized what the coup d'état was all about. Death, destruction, and chaos. Life was turned around for millions of people in Afghanistan. Our world shifted from one of happiness and security, to that of fear and instability.

Although my family had extended some extra benefits and security due to my father's position as a diplomat, there was still the looming fear that it could collapse at any moment. Leaving our house or spending time outside of the embassy compound was the worst. Nothing was guaranteed. The country went from a safe republic and turned into a massively chaotic struggle for survival. The uncertainty of tomorrow hung over everyone in Afghanistan.

My parents tried to be selective with the information they shared with me and my brother. They knew that knowing the severity of the situation we were in wouldn't sit well with a 9-year-old and a toddler. Despite their efforts, however, I saw the world around me with clear eyes. Though I was too young to understand the reason and politics behind the coup d'etat, I could see the life-threatening future we faced every day.

During this time, there were a few occasions when my father had left our home to travel to the embassy. Though both compounds were relatively safe, the journey there was unpredictable. Every time he left, I feared for his life. I imagined that every "goodbye" I said to him was the last one.

The streets were filled with secret police and soldiers that were pro-new government. They were given the authorization to shoot down anyone suspected of anti-government motives. There were no trials, no just ruling over whether what they perceived was true or not. It was turmoil and violence; neither of which needed reason for justifying the actions of the new government.

I remember stories my father used to tell us when he came back from traveling to work, or meeting people in the market. Those stories scared us to death.

He retold everything he witnessed in the aftermath of bombardments that would happen several days in a row. Houses would be torn apart, large holes carved the city streets, other embassies falling victim to these bombs. It all seemed unreal. I couldn't imagine the world he was explaining until I went out and saw the destruction for myself. I remember thinking over and over again that it could have just as easily been my family underneath all the rubble. It could have been my house that was bombed, my father's embassy that became the next target -- the uncertainty weighed heavily on me.

If I wasn't scared for my life every day, it would have seemed incredible how life could be so normal one day and then turn into a warzone the next. If only my childhood worries ended with the struggle at public school in Afghanistan. However, I wasn't fortunate to have a safe and secure childhood. I was thrown into utter disarray, uncertain whether my life was just beginning or if it was coming to an end.

Would I be able to say, "See you soon" and "Let's catch up next week?" to my neighbors and friends? Was it false hope to say such things or would I really be able to see them again? I had no control if I would even be alive tomorrow. The unpredictability of the future scared me, and I realized that life shouldn't be taken for granted. If today was your last day, what would you do to make it worthwhile?

This was just the first incident among so many others I've experienced that made me realize the gravitas of life. After the first coup d'états, there were two more I had lived through during my time in Afghanistan. Once my family moved back to Iran, I spent years surviving the turmoil during Iran's revolution along with the Iran and Iraq war. Between being bombarded by Iraq's fighter plane in Tehran and life in a refugee camp due to the fear of prosecution, I had no idea what day would be my last.

Looking back on my life now, I am surprised I have made it this far. The hope I held onto for a brighter tomorrow kept me going each day. In the end, I fought my way through life and settled in a safer place. I close my eyes every night knowing that the sun tomorrow will be peaceful.

My journey through life and the challenges I had to face, while terrifying in the moment, were obstacles that have led me to where I am today. I tried to keep my head up and have hope for a brighter future because life is filled with possibilities. Although it can be uncertain at times, there is no tomorrow without people to fill it. What you face isn't the end; it is a beginning to a future of striving and hoping.

Life is filled with troubles and injustice. No matter what you do or where you are, hope is the total enlightenment keeping you intact and pushing you forward to fight the next battle.

It is ironic that we fight such battles, both with ourselves and with the world. We try to hold the value of life above our heads in hope that it will lead us to a brighter future, but what happens when our arms strain under the pressure of fighting for tomorrow?

Keeping oneself intact is easiest in our youth. We are the most colorful as children and even with the hardships and struggles we face; we keep our dreams and hope close to our hearts. There is room in our lives for imagination and painting a picture of a bright future. No matter what our background may be or what situation we were in as a child, there is undoubtedly a moment in your childhood where your future was colored with the promise of a dream.

What do you want to be when you get older? This is a question that most of us come across during our childhood. Whether it is a question we think of or one that is brought up by the adults in our life, it is something important that we reflect on as a child.

As a child, you can be anything and everything, there is no version of yourself that you aren't able to envision. It is only as you get older that the colors in your life fade to muted renditions. Just like your vision, perhaps the hardships of life and your surroundings dampen your colors or completely abolish some of them. Maybe the future you've dreamed about gets trampled and your disheartenedness darkens the colors in your life. Whatever the reason, your colors change over the course of your life.

"Life is what happens when you're busy making other plans."
-John Lennon

Ultimately, your life is what you make of it. As you get older, *you* must define what colors are in your life and how you want to color your life. Nothing will change unless you make that change happen. If the people you hang out with live a life that contrasts with yours and that dulls the colors in your life, make the change. Surround yourself with people who will compliment your lifestyle and bring the color out in your life that you're seeking.

Within your group of friends, be the one who rises up among them and takes charge. Do what interest you while also taking initiative and leading your friends to follow. Feed them with suggestions and offer them ideas based on what you deem is the best course of action. As a society, we have become so comfortable being where we are in life. We are afraid of confrontation and failure, but we cannot achieve the life that we want if we are stagnant. Take charge of your life, who is in your life, and who you want to be within your community.

Start by letting the past stay in the past. There is no room for those dark and difficult times in your future. Give yourself the light and energy you need to carry forward and I promise you that people will start recognizing your shine. Those who are searching for joy and change in their life will be lured in by the glow you give off. Unlike those who live in the same bleak routine of life, wanting to change but being too scared of it, by taking a different path of light and enthusiasm, you harness an intelligence.

There are many people in the world who search for happiness through material gain, looking for *things* to satisfy them. Be it more money, the comfort of possession, indulgence in delicious food, or parading around with arm candy, it is dangerous to be too engrossed in the materialistic world. While these things could be a powerful compliment to the colors in your life, there is a fine line between balance and when we've lost ourselves in these desires.

Many believe that we can buy or attain happiness through what we give and what we receive. We are so focused on the world without that we live in the same, constant pattern of misunderstanding life. Though our actions may vary, it is the same habit taking different forms. As human beings, we collectively have a lack of awareness on how to live life and how to give life to others through colors and true values within the world. Society has evolved to put more importance on the material world. Many relationships we hold only scratch the surface, so it is easy to misinterpret what it means to have a colorful life and help others sustain the colors in their lives.

The pathway to living a colorful life is the key factor the majority of us miss. In our quest throughout life, we simply go from day to day, adding onto our dissatisfaction and worries. We are thwarted by the constant antagonizing idea that we might not be useful to society, despite whatever material gains we might have accumulated. These ideas and worries lead us to a colorless life full of doubt and uncertainty.

As with all things, there is a slice of truth underlying our worries. It isn't unless we involve ourselves in the service of others that our worries hold no weight. We cannot attain a mental peace of mind if we don't consciously work towards being an integral part of the lives of others. A selflessness and a need to help lies within all of us. It is natural to want to help those who are in need of service. The smallest amount of aid is not only received by those we help but also within ourselves.

It has become a stigma in society that service to others needs to be completely selfless. If you feel any amount of satisfaction or recognition, your actions immediately nullify the service that you've done or given. However, this idea isn't a healthy one and to discredit another's action is shameful in itself.

We cannot deny the delight we feel when we've helped another person. An immediate satisfaction and happiness washes over us when we see the smile rewarding our action. Extending a gesture, no matter how big or small of love to the sick, elderly, poor, children, or animals whenever needed is the best possible way for life to expand with color.

Do not relish in the praise you get for helping others but do relish in the delight you feel for simply knowing you did a good thing for another.

Life is colored by the service you give to others, and the more you give the more color your life will have.

HOW TO LIVE LIFE
There are three things that constitute life:

a) *knowing who you are first and foremost,*
b) *being someone worth the life you were given (or make an impact on the world),*
c) *and remembering you are not alone.*

In the routine of life, we find ourselves overwhelmed with busy schedules and surrounded by so many unnecessary burdens that weigh on us. It is hard to have a clear focus on how to live life when we are at the mercy of the circumstances that whirl around us, drawing our attention away. We focus on the materialistic world, and we chase after accumulating our gains. However, in doing so we forget what it means to live life, and as such, suffocating our potential and value.

Ultimately, it is *Human Desire* that destroys us. We build ourselves up, nurture dreams and futures, but in the end, we are the one that stands in our own way. The significance of life is to care for one another. We need to start speaking to and understanding those who are different from us or someone in need of help. Life doesn't revolve around you and thinking so is detrimental. Other people should not have to sacrifice their norms at your behest. The desire to find ways to abuse, exploit, and expect others to do things for us exists within everyone.

You can be the nicest person in the world, give back generously, and always step first onto the right path, but *Human Desire* isn't selective. You cannot choose to simply not have *Human Desire*; it festers within all of us, no matter how small. However, hope shall not be lost by this realization. Just as we work towards vision our whole life, we also need to work towards keeping our *Human Desires* at bay. Focus on abolishing arrogance from how you present yourself to others. Give back and pay forth. By taking these steps, we work towards living a better life.

Living in Japan, the work culture is quite severe. I have peers who have succumbed to the routine of unrelenting work and chasing monetary gain. Whether they are working for a corporation or for themselves, they drain the color out of their life by working it away. Long hours, weekends, extensive overtime, these people work with the idea that money is essential to having a healthy family and supporting loved ones.

While it may seem honorable to work and support loved ones through the comfort of money, there is a lack of nurturing in their life. They are working their life away, missing small moments in their life to appreciate the change in season or a change in their household.

Money can't buy everything and while it can be argued that money is one of the biggest factors that impact our lives, which doesn't always make it a good thing. While it could be used for positive reasons such as health, education, and even the food you consume, there is oftentimes a high possibility of it corrupting your life if used in excess or used carelessly. Money has always been a strong *Human Desire* and though it could relieve poverty, hunger, and many more great things, it can also get in the way of family and loved ones.

We are then faced with the question: if the value of life is adding color to it through various means, and *how* to live life is through giving back, then how do I not stray from the path? How can I make my life colorful?

When you are young, life seems so simple and clear. You don't have many possessions and the things you do have are at the mercy of your guardians. It is easier to give back without the weight of society watching you and creating a colorful life seems easy. You are young, healthy, full of vitality and future plans.

However, over time, we begin to complicate the simple things in life. The truth of the matter is: life is still as simple as it was when we were kids. Life has not changed; it is *you* who has changed. It is society that has made you believe that living a full life is more difficult. Life should be a breath of fresh air or young blooms after a long winter.

While we grow into adults, we begin to prohibit and restrain ourselves, diluting the colors of our life with it. We dull our own colors by trying to fit into the framework of conventions and constraints, but what is the point? We were full of life, joy, happiness, and laughter when we were children. We didn't think about what to eat, what to wear, what time to go to bed, we were simply content doing whatever it is that made us happy.

How can we get back to that life of blissful happiness? How do we erase the worry that has etched itself onto our foreheads and made our hairs gray?

Tips we can implement into our daily life so that it becomes easier and more joyful:

- Say hello to others, greet them when entering a shop, café or restaurant.
  - A simple gesture can have the biggest impact on both you and others. They won't forget the happiness you bestowed upon them, and you will feel lighter by just sharing kindness. *It brings color to everyone's life!*

- Travel without the worries of reality. Nearby or somewhere far, expand your horizons.
  - The people you meet and the cultures you come across will surely have different colors and patterns that'll add to your life.

- Be polite, well-mannered and considerate towards others.
  - Pay special attention to the relationships that are really important to you and be mindful of the directors in your life (loved ones, teachers, peer groups).

- Meditate and remind yourself what your purpose is in life and how fortunate you are to simply live.
  - Inhale a deep breath of yesterday and exhale your life today. Let something go and soften your eyes towards the prospects of tomorrow.

- Do not live in a materialistic bubble.

- o Focusing on a materialistic lifestyle is similar to a virus. It is all consuming. Save yourself, others and our planet by being more mindful.
- ■ Talk openly and without hesitation.
  - o It is hard for others to understand you if you do not express your feelings.
- ■ Do not overload yourself. Sleeping, eating, and exercising are vital rituals in life.
  - o You may work hard and fill your pockets with money but at the cost of struggling with other essential factors in life. Live and don't lose your own life.
- ■ Don't pretend and stop comparing yourself to others; envy will gradually destroy you.
  - o Our differences are what makes us a unique part of society. There isn't one person who is the epitome of humankind. Despite our differences, we can connect to one another through our cultural values, feelings and aspirations.
- ■ Maintain relationships with people who are close to you in spirit and complement you.
  - o In doing so, you can learn something new and useful from them and expand your horizons.
- ■ Unplug and set time aside for those around you.
  - o The digital world has become an integral part of daily life. It is easy to forget other important values in life when you're glued to a world you can access at your fingertips. Stop using your gadgets while your parents, kids and loved ones are around. Spending valuable time with them unplugged from

your devices. These moments won't ever come back. Cherish it with love and ears.

- Be wise about how and where to use your devices.
  - ○ Modern technology is designed to make your life easier but be wary of the consequences that you can encounter.
- Keep healthy relationships, especially with your loved ones.
  - ○ Regular contact and communication are important. Don't be scared to share your feelings and interact honestly.
- Finally, enjoy each moment while having fun creating a colorful personality.
  - ○ Just as a rainbow is full of color, so is life. Make your life full of rainbows.

"Although the road is never ending, take a step and keep walking, do not look fearfully into the distance… On this path, let the heart be your guide for the body is hesitant and full of fear."

-Rumi (Molana)

Life is filled with possibilities. You must challenge yourself in order to attain the life you want. To *make a difference* you first must act. Your life is your own just as your vision is your own. No one can walk your path for you, nor can they attain your vision for you. If you are too scared to take the first step, what is left of your life? Is there no vision? No happiness? No hope? How can you overcome your fear and seize the possibilities in front of you?

There are so many problems in life, both big and small, that need to be solved. Just because something is difficult doesn't mean that it isn't worth trying. Everyone is fighting their own battles, so you can't wait for someone else to battle yours. Make small victories today because who knows what tomorrow holds. The first step is always the hardest, but once you take it, you'll realize that vision, hope, happiness, courage is all possible with one small step.

Chapter 2
Importance of Family - Nearest and Dearest

When I was a child, my mother once told me that one clap isn't as powerful as the claps of many. No matter how strong you are or how capable you might be, you will always need people in your life who support you and lift you up. Vice versa, if you help one another, you'll be able to accomplish more than you know.

One person cannot do everything, and those who are adamant about clapping on their own will struggle through life. The sound of one clap is weaker than the sound of many. Instead of competing with others and trying to see who can make the loudest sound, work together and clap in unity. For if you do, the reward of working together will be more than either person could accomplish in working alone.

My mother has always guided me to do better and be a better person. She has built me to hold the morals and values I have today. She has given me life lessons that I hold onto in my darkest times.

Parents are the most important pillars of our lives. They are the ones who hold up the structure of family and show us the path to the future. They impart words of wisdom onto us and feed us with love, hope, and promises of a brighter future. Our parents establish the foundation of our relationships, love, self-development, and how we conduct ourselves in society. They are the most precious gift in our lives, just as we are to our children. Nothing can replace the bonds we make with our family. Mothers and fathers breathe life into us. They help us up when we fall down, instill meaning into our lives and inspire hope within us.

Parents play the most important role in the family. It is a parent's duty to teach their children important aspects in life and prepare them for a bright future. However, there are certain capacities that each parent has. 1.) There are families who come from wealthier backgrounds that *have* the capacity to ensure their child gets a bright future. However, there are some who are distracted by their wealth. This hinders parental roles, and due to laziness and a lack of awareness about the world, the child isn't given a good start to life. 2.) In contrast, there are parents who are less privileged, unable to send their children off to a good school or extracurriculars. Despite wanting to provide their kids with the best future, they simply cannot because of the lack of capacity they have. However, despite lacking financial abilities, they provide their children with life lessons to make up for what they cannot financially afford. 3.) Lastly, there are parents who *have* the wealth and capacity, yet the world around them prevents them from preparing their children. There are many factors that might inhibit a parent's capacity, from an unstable environment to societal impediments.

Despite a parent's capability, they all try their hardest to give their children the best future they can have. There is an unconditional love between parents and children, a family is built on this love and creates deep ties that attach us to sacrifices we are willing to make for our family and the lengths we would go to make them happy. Family is filled with colors, however, their acceptance of you has no color; it is pure with love and affection.

Yet, the importance of family has changed in many ways over the generations. With the advancement of technology and society, the structure of family has weakened. The world grows bigger, and cities grow larger, however, at the same time, the world is also shrinking. With the advancement of technology, science, and transportation we have the ability to be much more connected than ever. Yet, despite the ease, we lose touch with one another and forget what it is like to connect with each other.

Before, children used to live with their parents until they got married, though some even lived with them afterwards, as well. Family used to be a tight knit society that was stabilized by traditional roles and beliefs that have changed drastically over the century. Now, it is easier for children to leave the nest. Independence from your family is easier to gain and life away from your family only takes one click of a button. Family has become second to other aspects in life and as we get older, we find that it is easier to disconnect ourselves from those who have raised us and nurtured us.

Take the status of family in Japan, as an example. Japan is renowned all over the world for its modernized advancements, but also its traditional culture. However, even Japan has changed over the past century, despite being perceived as having a "traditional culture." With major cities like Tokyo and Osaka growing more populated and modernized, the idea of work, business, and climbing the corporate ladder comes first in life while family and loved ones come second in most cases.

The idea of keeping a healthy family is stemmed through money and living a comfortable life consists of paying for anything that needs to be fixed and whatever problem arises. Many families like this turn to wealth in order to save their relationships or provide them a better life, but money isn't going to be there for you when you are sick and injured. There is only so much money to be made, and once it is all gone, who do you have to turn to afterwards?

A King in the eyes of his daughter;
and the whole world in the eyes of the Father -unknown source

Robert Brault, an American opera tenor singer once said, *"Enjoy the little things, for one day you may look back and realize they were the big things."*

Being alive is colorful and bright in itself. The value of life is something that should be cherished in each and every moment, yet we forget how lucky we are to be alive and to be loved by the people around us. We don't need the whole world in order for us to be happy, we just need that one person that sees *us* as their whole world to share happiness.

The father and daughter above have only each other and the clothes on their back, yet the love and joy radiating between them is something to strive towards. You don't need to have the whole world because your whole world could be standing right in front of you, looking up to like nothing else in the world matters. It is important to spend time with loved ones and those you hold close. They play an important role in your life, and it is important to remember that you wouldn't be where you are today if it weren't for them. Tomorrow isn't promised, so live today with brightness in your heart and spread it to others who may not bathe in the light like you.

Tips and reminders between Nearest and Dearest to keep them closer and stronger relationship:

- Don't forget your role in each relationship
- Love each moment life has to offer and acknowledge what you have received from your parents
- Don't let go of the chance to hug or kiss your loved ones - moments are fleeting and won't ever come back
- Be as affectionate as you can toward your parents/children and partner, show them how much you care with your words, not just buying their love
- Don't hesitate to show your affection to your loved ones, no matter their age; use words like "Love," "Darling," "I miss you," "I am proud of you," and "my sunshine"
- When speaking to your toddlers, meet them eye to eye. Don't talk down to them, but show them that you are on the same level as them when they are trying to express something important to them
- Words of admiration and encouragement are the key to building their confidence and courage
- Make your children feel like you are their best friend and

buddies - someone they can confide in and trust
- Try to be creative and challenge yourself to create something new to play with them

Making a *living* isn't the same thing as making a *life*. Don't sacrifice family for money. The most important thing in life is to build a healthy family through love, compassion, ethics, and quality time because when you are at the lowest point in your life, it will be your family to shine a light down on you and raise you out of the darkness. It is without a doubt that we tend to forget and take for granted the importance and magnitude of life and how soon it can end.

Do not educate your children to be a robot, work hard so that they can be successful and rich, educate them to be courageous, be worthy people, to have hope and strive. Teach them to be a tree that moves in the wind and not a leaf that easily falls at the slightest breeze.

After years of working with children and youth in Japan, I noticed that young people have so much to offer to the world, yet there is always something holding them back. They had so much they wanted to share but they struggled to express themselves and communicate with others. Over the years, I've realized that communication and interaction has become a major issue in Japan and for the younger generation. Sometimes the consequences of a lack of communication can have life-threatening repercussions, especially when mental health isn't addressed properly.

Within the Japanese seniority structure, it can be hard for the youth to stand up and speak their mind. It can be frustrating to hold back ideas and accept the words and directions of those who are older. From a young age, it has been ingrained in children to hold their tongue around their elders and cope with their problems on their own. However, while culture plays a huge role towards the youth problem in Japan, it is important not to downplay the significance of healthy communication.

We first learn how to communicate through our parents. It is mimicking their gestures, sounds, and words that we begin to build our own standard for communication. However, it can be hard to communicate with our family as we get older and our ideas, personality, and identity change. We learn how to communicate through school, our friends, and media, however, that begins to take away our communication with our family. It has become normal to communicate less with your family as you get older and establish your own life but limiting your communication with those who have known you all your life shouldn't be normalized.

Communication is important and we shouldn't be ashamed or afraid of sharing our negative emotions or thoughts with those we are closest to. Just as we want to share our joy and happiness with our loved ones, we need to normalize sharing our negative emotions, too. Holding back a part of yourself that is struggling and trying to find the light all on your own will only dampen your colorful life. Everyone is full of color, and they impart a part of their colors onto you. By communicating your sufferings, you are welcoming a chance for light at the end of your tunnel.

However, not all of us are lucky enough to hold onto our parents and closest confidants throughout our childhood. Death, turmoil, estrangement, there are a plethora of reasons why we might get separated from our family at a young age. It isn't always what we want or need, but there are situations beyond our control that take them away from us. We need to cherish the moments we can freely communicate with our parents and family because we never know how limited our time might be.

After graduating high school at the age of sixteen, a couple years early, I had to plan and start my adult life. However, as a Baha'i in Iran, there was no future for me to continue education. The Islamic Government of Iran prohibited us, the Baha'i, from going to university or working. It was the law, yet none of us was allowed to legally leave Iran either. We were not allowed to hold passports, gain higher education, or apply ourselves in a proper work environment.

I was faced with a future I didn't know how to attain. It was my parents who helped me plan and prepare for a future where I could actually have a chance at success. However, the preparations they made for my future were something I never thought I would have to face. I will never forget the lengths I had to go through to secure a future for myself. Everything happened so fast. There was no time for hesitation or second guessing.

In a matter of 48 hours, I had to prepare myself to leave everything I have ever known behind. I was to become a refugee. I couldn't understand the full spectrum of the journey I was about to set out on or the toll leaving my family would have on me. My sister was only 4 years old at the time and she was my world. I tried not to think about when I would see her again or when I would see my parents or brother again.

48 hours came and went so fast. *Believe in yourself and hope that we may one day meet each other again. Life is much bigger.* Those were the words of wisdom my mother and father imparted on me that day. I left them for a better future, an uncertain future and I held onto those words tightly as I began my long journey.

Over the course of seven nights and eight days, I was led by two smugglers through the desert and Rocky Mountains along with five other Baha'is who have been through similar trauma. All of us had gone through some severe hardship in Iran, and all of us decided to flee for our lives and try to build a future somewhere brighter. Among our group, three were older cousins of mine who had suffered so much just because of their belief. During those eight days and seven nights, my mind sharpened and I realized just how important my family was to me. Despite arguments we might have had, disagreements, opposite opinions or views, my family was the dearest thing to me. I needed to have hope even though there was no one there to encourage it.

After my long, tiring journey, I spent the next two and a half years as a refugee in Pakistan trying to attain the better life, I was sent off to find.

Though I tried to harbor hope of my own, when I looked for someone to lean on and support me, the people who have been there my whole life were gone. My family, who had nurtured me, inspired me, loved me, and gave me hope were no longer there. I was filled with hopelessness and a deep sadness that I had never felt before. I kept thinking about my family and realizing how much they had done to protect me as a child. Now that I was on my own, fleeing for my life, I knew the sacrifices they went through to keep me safe.

Even though I went through many tough challenges so early on in life, I was very fortunate to have a family that was always there for me. I wondered if it wasn't my density to have a simple life, but one that swung me from different extremities. My life was colorful, to be sure, but having my family there, standing alongside me gave the colors of my struggle new meaning.

Though my path had been a difficult one, I had never lost hope and had unwavering faith in building my life. Witnessing how my mother and father survived through extremely difficult times had taught me how to fight and keep my head up, even when I wanted to give up. Their presence strengthened my hope and my resolve.

However, when I had to leave my family at the age of sixteen, my hope wavered. I faced major pain and trauma. Saying goodbye to them and not knowing when I would see them again tore me apart.

It took me a while to realize that no matter what happened or how bad life might seem today, the world still goes round, and tomorrow would be a full, new day. The bad days don't last forever, and the trouble you are faced with will disappear with time, no matter how terrible it seems.

Courage is the key to overcoming the darkness and bad days. Be strong, have faith and think about all the good and happy memories you had, because they are sure to come again. Use this as a motivator to keep us intact and give us the strength to move forward. Hope played a significant role in my life, more than I could ever imagine. Though everyone has a different path in life and mine was quite treacherous, we should remember the hardships we have been through and how far we have made it since then.

Those surreal events that you want to forget or wish desperately to re-do will make you braver and more thoughtful about your surroundings. Use the dark and painful incidences you have faced in life to your advantage and think about what you can do to help others. How we utilize our lowest point in life is up to us. The darkness that haunts us and the hopelessness that brings us down are moments where we have the opportunity to build a life that could lead us to something greater than we could ever imagine.

However, we must not forget that hope isn't a one-way street. Just as everything in life, there is a circularity to how we live life. The colors in our lives aren't created from us, but from those around us and how *we* are created when we interact with them. Don't forget that those around you also have darkness within them and that there are times when their life is faced with hopelessness. By showing them love and compassion where we can, we share our hope and optimism.

"You are the sum total of everything you've ever seen, heard, eaten, smelled, been told, forgot - it is all there. Everything influences each of us, and because of that I try to make sure that my experiences are positive."

-Maya Angelou

Regardless of your relationship with your parents, whether they are near or far, you'll miss them immensely when they are gone from your life. The importance of family is so much more than we can truly ever realize. We take our family for granted every day because they are a constant rock in our life. We think that they will always be there for us whenever we need them, but that is not always true.

Our lives and the people in our lives are so much more than we recognize. Instead of filling life with bad emotions and experiences, taking out our anger and dissatisfaction on those closest to us, focus on the beauty in the world. Before it's too late.

Revel in the feeling of love and being loved, acknowledge the value of family, and say "I love you" to those you hold close to your heart. Be thankful for those who made you the person you are today and gave your life. There might come a time in life where you will have to throw caution into the wind and go down a path in life that you never imagined. Treasure the time you have now instead of waiting until it is too late.

As we go forth on our path towards vision, as we strengthen our bonds with hope, we must remember that our lives are circular. What we give is what we get in return, and the roundness of our lives affects those around us as well. It isn't just family that gives us hope and colors our lives, but many other directors we treasure. Friends are the family we chose, and we must remember that when our family doesn't have the capacity to support us, it is our friends we turn to next.

The bonds we make in life need to be strong, no matter who we make them with. If they are important in our lives, it is important that we show them and remind them how much we appreciate what they give us.

As His Holiness Dalai Lama once said
"Give the ones you love wings to fly, roots to come back, and reasons to stay.

Chapter 3
Friendship - The Bonds we Choose

*F*riends didn't have a particular role earlier in my childhood. It wasn't until I was sixteen and alone for the first time away from family as a refugee in Pakistan that I started to realize the importance of friendship. Without my family to support me, I turned to others and began to confide in them. Every day was different and the people I saw and met changed like the season, but I was always meeting new people who were in the same situation I was in. Everyone was facing their fears and the life that led them to the refugee camp was filled with hardship as well.

I interacted and learned from hundreds of other refugees and each interaction I had with them made me feel safe and not so alone. The friends I made became my family and major directors in my life that helped to develop my vision. There were innumerable times when they treated me as if I were their true siblings. They would take me under their wing and guide me to a brighter future filled with hope rather than despair.

Similarly, I also thought of them as my brothers or sisters. Their encouragement, hope, support, and love came to me in a time when my whole world changed. There was so much uncertainty in my life at this time and they helped ease my burden of the unknown.

Our room - Refugee time in Pakistan - 1986

If it wasn't for the people I met at the refugee camp, I wouldn't be the person I am today. They helped build me as a person and raised me up when I was down. They created a strong, independent, mature person who was able to leave the refugee time with hope rather than despair. They were valuable friends who stood beside me and taught me how to live life and how to make sacrifices for more important values in life, all the while showing me their sincerity and caring for me deeply.

I created bonds with a few of these men who became brothers to me when it wasn't possible to see my actual brother. The other refugees who surrounded me daily were my family when I grew homesick and worried about the welfare of my parents and siblings. We would sleep like sardines on the floor, walk hours to the town in order to get supplies we needed, play football, cards and talk with each other. We were all suffering in some way or another -- most of us had left those we cared about behind and sought comfort in the company of one another. We were friends in a dire time of need and support.

Before I fled Iran, my brother, Navid, was the closest friend I had. He and I built so many memories together and shared a lot of experiences that changed us through our childhood. Though not all of the moments we shared were in happy and carefree times, we cherished the times we spent playing and running together. We laughed, sang, fought, and protected each other. Ever since he was a toddler, I was amazed by his determination and intelligence when it came to things that he wanted to achieve. He observed life differently than other kids I met during our childhood. I was glad to be his friend and we gained so much from our precious journey together.

However, when I left Iran, my brother was only 11 years old. There was so much that we never got the chance to do and so many memories we never got the chance to make together. While my 4-year-old sister was my whole world, my brother was my dearest companion. Having to leave brought me so much pain and sorrow. He was my best friend, and no matter how much I tried to keep my family at the forefront of my thoughts and remember all the beautiful memories I had made, the thought of never being able to see my best friend again wore me thin. It wasn't for over a decade when I would get to see him again. Although times have changed and we grew into different people, we were able to build a totally new friendship. Our understanding of one another and of life had changed. He isn't just family, but a friend that is irreplaceable.

Establishing Friendship:
- *To make a good friend is not easy*
- *To keep a good friend is very challenging*
- *To lose a good friend is unbearable*

Dr. Riaz Ghadimi

In 1990, I was fortunate to attend Dr. Riaz Ghadimi, a highly distinguished Baha'i, during one of his talks in Toronto, Canada. The three points above were topics he had talked about, and they had resonated so deeply within me. I have not and will not ever forget his words nor the power of his talk. He had enlightened my thoughts and inspired me forward.

After his talk, I was left with the pressing question: how do I make a good friend, and after building that bond, how do I protect and maintain that friendship? By the time I had heard this talk, I had already made many friends that changed my life for the better, but I had also lost so many friendships I made over the years. I had lost the bonds I made with people over the lack of communication, distance, turmoil, trouble, etc., so if I was going to connect with new people, open myself up and learn to accept them into my world, how could I deal with the mental and moral effect that it would have on me after losing them?

The answer to big questions like these has never been easy, but if there is one thing that I learned in life it is that *we are never alone*. There might be times or situations in life that make us feel utterly isolated, but there are always people around who are willing to help. Life is nothing but a map of obstacles that we have to overcome to move forward.

Whenever I hit an obstacle that was hard to overcome, I always looked up at the blue sky. Each cloud paints an incredible picture that lasts only a moment. They are blown away, their shape changes form, they swell with rain, but they are beautiful in that moment. Tomorrow it'll be a different cloud with different beauty, but right now, you exist in the beauty of today. Your life is the same in that you are surrounded by so many beautiful people that go and go in your life. They all mark a moment in your life that can be fleeting yet impactful. It is up to you to hold tight to their guidance and the impact they had on your life. It is up to you to utilize what you learned so that the moment doesn't go to waste.

Remember that friendship is a process and a journey. To meet and build strong friendships, you need to put *time and effort* into your friends. Friendship is only as strong as you make it. Putting time and effort in solidifies a strong foundation to build a relationship on. It also requires lots of *sacrifices* to be made. Human beings are malleable. We have our vision and values that set us in our way, but it's the friends around us that make us more colorful. They add new knowledge and ideas to our world, and we change who we are with who we want to be.

It is important to make *compromises* and have *good communication* to feed our friendships. We cannot expect our friends to follow us blindly. It is a give and take relationship that is stronger with communication and understanding of the other person's values and beliefs. If we don't respect our friends, how can we expect them to respect us? Lastly, it is what we do to *keep* and *fight* for our friendships that really matters. If the bond you make isn't worth the fight, then it isn't as strong as you thought. You need to work hard to keep your friends and value them.

However, it isn't just *how to keep* a good friend that matters, but *how to choose* good friends that make keeping them easier.

"A wise friend laughs once, but an unwise friend laughs thousands of times." This wisdom was imparted on me at a young age from my mother. When we are young, we are easily changed by the world and the people around us. Though the friends we have at a young age might be faces and names we don't remember, it is important to look for the friends that will laugh with you and not at you. It is important to create friendships that will build us up and not break us down,

When we are young, it is easy to make friends. Our worlds are small, and our interests are as fickle as the weather. We become friends with someone who smiles at us or someone we share laughs with, but as we get older our world broadens and our vision broadens with it. It is harder to make friends as we get older because we know the path we want to walk on, and it takes more than a smile and a laugh to create deep bonds.

Time and effort play an integral part in who we meet on our path to the future. Since our priorities and lifestyles change over the years, our approach to meeting valuable friends also changes. As such, when we make friends, it is important to identify and understand who we are becoming friends with. We need to choose those who walk on or near the same path as us. Making sure that our character and vision aligns is important.

To a junior and high school student, friendship is much purer and more unconstrained by societal pressures. When you're a teenager, your friendship revolves around school projects, recreational activities, games and young love. It isn't until you get to higher education when the meaning of friendship begins to shift. There is still a tie to school, but it is during this time friendship plays a more constructive role in building your adult life and career. Higher education is the time to find yourself and build your whole world of exploration and fun.

A very wise and close friend once told me that he categorizes friends and those around him into a four-zone pattern.

Zone 1: Those closest to you. This zone includes people in your life that are connected to you by DNA. This being your parents, children, siblings, relatives - those that are willing to sacrifice the world for you, love you unconditionally, and vice versa.

Zone 2: Your best and closest friends. This is where our solid and strongest friendships exist. Those who understand you and your past, who support your life, career, failures, and joy. These people are the ones in your life for the long run. They are not tied to you by blood nor are they bought with your money. They stay with you because they genuinely love and care for you. These are the friendships you turn to when you are at the lowest point in your life. They will never leave you when you face hardship but will help you with nothing but sincerity.

Zone 3: Those you've built a good foundational friendship with. These are friends you've met through school, work or other activities. Perhaps you know them, and you enjoy their company, but you aren't well familiar with them or their past, and you don't share the same vision. They may not have the same lifestyle as you and not value the same things as you do, but you are close enough that you can count on them and share your ideas and aspirations for your future. You can share your success and your problems, but the comfort and understanding they provide is limited.

Zone 4: These are the people you meet casually, who you don't feel obligated to meet. There is a potential to build a stronger relationship, but the stability of it is uncertain. This friendship isn't based on mutual value, vision, or thinking of the future, it is simply built out of unbound enjoyment. They are mainly looking at how to utilize or benefit from you in one way or another, and perhaps you feel the same way. They are just a means to an end and in most cases, they come and go. There are no strings attached to this friendship and no pressure to make or maintain a stronger bond.

From these zones, 2 and 3 play the biggest role in your life's path. While Zone 1 is important in its own regard, Zones 2 and 3 are the bonds we choose to make and not the ones we are born into. They play a key role in how your future unfolds and though there is no one who can live your life for you, they heavily influence your life and career.

"In the end, we will remember not the words of our enemies, but the silence of our friends."

\- Martin Luther King, Jr.

It is better to have quality over quantity when it comes to who your friends are. Having two or three close friends with strong values, positive energy, thoughtfulness, and joy will color your life and give it a clearer direction. Having strong bonds with your friends is much more meaningful than having hundreds of friends you cannot trust or confide in.

It is important to evolve with your friends rather than apart from them.

As we get older, we change as people. Our situation, background, learning and values in life lead us towards different paths. We are all unique and different, and though we might resonate with our friends, change within both of us is inevitable. As such, we need to work hard to understand and communicate with those we cherish and treasure. Once we've established strong bonds, we need to work towards keeping them.

We have many friends throughout our lives that come and go. Just because these friends are no longer in our lives doesn't mean that they were bad friendships or that they didn't mean anything. A good friend knows your life stories and what you are going through, but the best friend is part of your life and a main character who has written your life script. Everyone is different with different values. What you gained from the friendships that didn't last is the knowledge of people who you don't click well with. You cannot force a friendship with a person just because you want a friend. You have to find and create a bond with someone who carries the same values and understanding as you. Not everyone has been in your shoes or has lived a similar life to you. Some people might not have the same capacity for friendship as you do, and others have a vastly different cultural or career background as you. However, if you are patient and willing to open yourself up, then a strong friendship filled with color, joy, and laughter will surely come your way.

"For beautiful eyes look for the good in others; for beautiful lips speak only words of kindness; and for poise, walk with the knowledge that you are never alone."

-Audrey Hepburn

Friends have a very special place in my life. I was very blessed to have made so many invaluable bonds throughout my teenage years and into my early adulthood. It wasn't just the refugee period where I made friends, but my life in Canada, after being a refugee, and in the United States, England, and Switzerland when I began my higher education journey. I've come so far from my arrival in Halifax, Canada in 1988 where I began learning how to live and survive by myself. From my time of hopelessness in Guelph, Canada when I struggled to find the path to my vision and tried to survive school. After 13 years of living, growing, learning, and becoming an adult, I finally reunited with my family in Australia for a short period. While fundamentally the same, I was a completely different person who saw the world through different eyes. I was no longer the frightened, young teenager they sent off with hopes of finding and securing a future, I was now a man who had striven towards his vision and made a better life for himself.

While my parents had nurtured, cared, and shaped who I was going to be as a child, as an adult, it was my friends who have helped me hone into the person I am today. Without their guidance, caring, and the sincerity of their friendship, I would not have reached my goals and I would have lost hope along the way.

However, having a good, strong friendship could be difficult at times. Friendship and companionship are something many people look for in life, but it is hard making new friends. Making a new friend means that you have to be vulnerable and let someone new into your world. The bond in a friendship is different from a family bond. Family bonds are something you're born into, they are different with each person and mean different things, but a bond in a friendship is created through trust and respect.

Tips for making and maintaining lasting friendships:

- Patience: do not rush to make a friend, trust that they will come
  - Build your own circle of friends and trust - if you are capable

- A true friend does not want you for your money/wealth
  - Strong friendships are more about giving rather than taking

- Be honest and true with your friends but keep healthy distance since everyone changes due to their priorities and lifestyle
  - Don't be afraid to make sacrifices along the way to build a solid friendship - but *evaluate* the sacrifices that you are making first

- Friends have the ability to bring your life into the light or darkness; build friendships that are on the same page as you
  - Do not let your friends control you in a way that could destroy your real value and importance of life and family

- A true friend and strong friendship are a treasure of a lifetime; don't let that get away from you easily
  - Put more time and energy into those who are special to you

- Listen more and share your true feelings and thoughts - these are the moments that will pass us by if we let them
  - Communicate with your friends often - not just when you need something

- Express your feelings by using words, writing, touch, and interaction -- it is not enough to buy their friendship

➢ Make sure you are there for them, especially in hard times

▪ Don't be afraid to disagree with your friend, you are two different people after all, but keep your values and boundaries in check

➢ Healthy arguments that stem from mutual respect is welcomed to building a stronger relationship

▪ Accept the changes that come with friendship. Everyone changes throughout life, especially as we get older, mature, and build our own families

➢ Have the capacity to forgive and let go to the extent that it doesn't hurt or encroach on your life and values

Friends can come from anywhere. They can come when you least expect it or when you need it the most. Friendship can be built in any space and time, there are no conditions to friendship and creating a bond with another human being. True and strong friendships are treasures of a lifetime. Nothing can replace the bond that is made between two people who love and care for each other like family.

It is from these bonds of friendship and family that we build the values of our lives. These bonds give us hope for a better life and a better future. The foundation of our happiness begins with these people who give color to our lives, though are the ones responsible to build on the foundation they give us. To pursue happiness and a more colorful life, we must first understand the value of happiness and work hard not to be blinded by obstacles that will threaten to take our happiness away.

Chapter 4
The Value of Happiness - Pursue it, Don't Lose it

Since the beginning of time, humans have been searching for happiness in their life. Some people attain happiness throughout their life's path, but even so, they might not recognize it. In the end they wondered if they were happy or if they missed the chance. Others wonder what it *truly* means to be happy. Just as every human being is unique, so is each person's view of happiness. Regardless, many have also misjudged the facts about this important value of life, *the enlightenment filled with joy.*

Does happiness belong to the present or is it eternal? How would we attain happiness if we do not truly understand what makes us happy? Life without it would be shrouded in darkness, would it not? Above all else, happiness comes from within you and lasts forever. It gives you the utmost satisfaction and brings about an unforgettable feeling that you can't help but want to share with others, especially loved ones and those closest to you.

Happiness is what we find when we work towards our vision; questions we've accumulated, the directors in our lives that help us along, and the trials we face to reach our life-long goal. On our path towards vision, we find happiness, and having hope makes it possible to strive towards it. Ultimately, happiness starts and ends with you.

Even if we cannot truly understand the meaning of happiness or the complexity of the emotion, we do recognize a sliver of happiness when we eat our favorite meal, are rewarded for an accomplishment, make those close to us feel happy, when we've built a life that we had always dreamed of, and so many more incidences that happens in our day-to-day life. Happiness isn't the reward for completing your life and all your life goals, it is something that builds up along the way.

Furthermore, we need to remind ourselves of the first time we have felt utter and complete happiness. We need to remember those who were the directors of our happiness and how it is a blessing to have these people in our lives. These directors in our lives have had a huge role and influence in our happiness. Even if we didn't realize it at the time, it is important that we realize it now. Without them and their ambiance and encouragement, we won't be able to reach the highest level of happiness that we seek.

We are all the colors of life - we live together in harmony to make this world more beautiful and give happiness to everyone.

Happiness has millions of colors, reasons, and influences. It isn't conditioned to exist only once, nor is it conditional. Happiness is more than words can express and it colors your life in vivid strokes. In our lifetime, we search for this transcendent feeling and even though we fight and strive towards our happiness every day, some of us might not fully reach it or be satisfied with what we have attained.

Our world has become so small and closed off sometimes that we forget that living the life we have and breathing on this extraordinary planet filled with thousands of languages, cultures, religions, rituals is a piece of happiness in itself. The world is filled with so many possibilities and opportunities; filled with so many colors that it is amazing and breathtaking to just be apart and witness the beauty of a world as impossible as ours.

My slice of happiness is being alive to experience how others succeed, bringing joy and comfort.

Some days are more difficult than others to believe that happiness exists. When it gets gloomy outside, it can be hard to remember that the sun will shine again. It is okay to be sad and filled with unhappy emotions. It is okay to let yourself go and forget the world. But just as the sun burns away the clouds, we, too, must burn away our negativity and fight to live another day in search of happiness.

My life was never simple or straight forward. Along with my parents and siblings, we struggled early on in life and learned that our path towards the future was going to be one with many obstacles. There are millions of people all over the world who are born and raised in peaceful neighborhoods, who've gone to kindergarten, junior high, and high school in the same town or country. These people then go onto higher education, secure a job, get married, buy a house, and then retire. It is a simple structure and routine that a huge portion of the population follows.

However, there are also millions of people that aren't so lucky to be born into such an environment. Though every struggle is different, it is a struggle, nonetheless. Unfortunately, my story falls in the latter category. As I've spoken about in previous chapters, my life was filled with so many challenges that my family and I had no choice but to accept. We had to live with and understand that these struggles were simply a part of our life. Despite our not-so-simple struggles, we still sought out happiness. Even when life kicked us down, we still dreamed of being happy and we wondered every day what true happiness would look and feel like.

Perhaps hardship will always define our lives and the lives of people like me -- the lives of those struggling. Some may even say it is our destiny to live in such a way, but even so, each human being deserves to have happiness, no matter how fleeting or short lived.

An Afghan born, only to bear witness to war and hardship; to grow and die with the concept that we will never experience peace and comfort in this lifetime. A Palestinian kid who grew up through war and strife, never seeing the bright side to life but always struggling every day to live for a tomorrow. Underprivileged children in India and the Philippines who are born and raised in slumps. Happiness evades them because the struggle to live consumes their thoughts; not sufficient access to food, clean water, education, health supplies, and the list goes on.

If every person on this planet deserves a shot at happiness, then why are there millions of people struggling to survive, deprived of a path to a healthy and happy life?

Even though I led a life of hardship and struggle, faced many coups, wars, and turmoil, lived as a refugee, and grew up away from my family, I was still lucky enough to find happiness between all the rubble that had accumulated in my life.

The most vivid memory of happiness in my life was my reunion with my parents and siblings. After 13 years of living and growing without my family near, without any way to contact them, and while they were going through their own struggles and hardship in Iran, I was able to finally meet them again. It was like I was stepping out of a dream and back into reality. The absence between us swelled to unmeasurable heartache. My sister was 4 when I had left and 17 when I reunited with her. My brother was 10 when I left and 23 when I saw him again. My parents, who guided me when I was younger, encouraged me when I was down, and gave me a future, were now older and wiser. I was much changed as well. I had my own stories of suffering just as they had theirs, but despite it all, we were happy. A family, now whole, filled with happiness in spite of it all.

Happiness. A simple word that carries a complexity of emotion.

My happiness was compounded by my struggles and sufferings. After I fled Iran, leaving my family behind, I spent two years as a refugee in Pakistan. I was very fortunate to be welcomed into Canada where I was given the opportunity to begin a new life. Although I was given the opportunity to embark on a journey that would mark the *Take Off* phase of a new chapter in my life, I was alone. I was a teenager in a country I have never visited, and I was alone. Though the struggles in Canada were different from Iran or Pakistan or Afghanistan, I lived an unstable life without durable guidance, void of protection from loved ones or family.

Like millions of refugees and immigrants being forced to leave their home and their loved ones, I had to find where I belonged in this world. I had to create a new life with my own two hands, mapping out and envisioning a way to build my life so it wouldn't crumble again. I was faced with a task no child should ever be faced with. As so many before me, and so many to come, I was taken away from family, traditions, friends, and my native tongue. It is hard to find happiness when everything you've ever known has been taken away from you. Despite the opportunities you've been given, sometimes the loss is too overwhelming.

Even though it was a hard transition in my life, I was still grateful for everything Canada had done for me and what a life in Canada meant. Countries such as Canada, Australia, Sweden, Germany, New Zealand and a few others, care and sympathize with the struggles of refugees and immigrants. These countries give you a new home and an opportunity to start again when your whole world seems bleak and colorless. Canada's immigration and support was invested in my wellbeing and integration into my new environment was undoubtedly a blessing. I am and forever will be indebted to the country for what I have become.

The burden of the loss I had taken and felt so wholly was alleviated by Canada's well-established foundation and the support the government offered me. I felt secure and safe for the first time in a long time. Although I was without the ones dearest to me and I was very anxious about continuing a life in Canada, I was able to become happy. I was given the factors I needed to appreciate what I had and what was offered to me in my time of need.

After over a decade of living in Canada and growing into a young man, I pursued my vision, passion, and happiness by continuing my education abroad. Though I still had a hole in my heart, I established a life where I could be happy, safe, and secure.

Within the 13 years I was away from my family, I was only able to talk with my parents once or twice a year through letters and rarely a phone call, especially in the first few years. This was very difficult for me since we were all very close. Before separating from my family, we would talk together often, and they were my closest confidant. Despite communicating with them occasionally, there were still times when I worried that something might have happened to them. It would give me some relief when I would hear from relatives from time to time, telling me that my parents were doing well.

It wasn't until my parents finally got their passports returned to them from the government in Iran that they were finally able to contact me on their own. Hearing from them and learning that they were moving to Australia where my brother, Navid, had immigrated a few years ago had softened a worry that had eaten at me for years. Knowing that they would finally be safe and that my family could have together once again brought me great joy. I decided to pack my suitcase and visit them.

In the summer of 1998, I was finally able to see my family again. In the Australian airport I suddenly realized what it meant to be overcome with happiness. All the friends I made along the way who gave me hope, the opportunities I was fortunate to have, the directors in my life motivating me towards my vision, and finally, my family. My family was the missing piece of my *true* happiness. Though they were present in my childhood, I didn't realize what I had until I had lost it all.

My compounded struggles in building a life without the support of my family had created an indescribable feeling of happiness within me. I was happy pursuing a higher education, and

I was able to build happiness during my time in Canada but being reunited with my family filled that hole in my heart that didn't allow me to be *truly* happy.

Although my life was a far cry from normal, and far different than what I had ever imagined, I learned and discovered how I could be happy. I learned that true happiness is the feeling of electricity that courses through your body and makes you feel like your heart will explode. It is something that changes you and gives you a whole new outlook on life. *It is your story, and the discovery of your own self is happiness.* It all begins with *you.* You are the one who will flourish, and in your time of flourishing, you will enlighten and empower others - just as others have done unto you. You are the one who designs and makes the changes in your life. The people you've met and the situations you've been in color your life, but it is what you do with all that color that matters. These colors combine with happiness and enlightenment, creating meaning for your life and propelling you to a brighter future.

"Happiness is when what you think, what you say, what you do are in harmony."

-Mahatma Gandhi

Take a moment to just breathe. What do you hear? What do you see or smell? What small victories have you accomplished today and what have been some situations where you accepted defeat? Be present in this moment and try to remember what it is that makes you happy? Is it something you are feeling now? Do you relish the taste of coffee in the morning? Does the quietness of the night bring you comfort? What are small parts of your everyday life that make you happy?

While there are moments of happiness that are more blatant than others, we have to remember that happiness comes in all shapes and sizes. Even if there is chaos all around us, just having a slice of comfort and happiness is enough to fight for more. What are your values in your life? Who are the friends and family that give you hope? Happiness is lost without hope. If we don't hope for a better tomorrow, how can we hope for happiness? Remember the small moments of happiness in your life and hope that this transcendent feeling will always be a part of your life.

Those who love you will never leave you, even if they have a hundred reasons to give up, they will always find that one reason to hold on.

I found happiness in my son's laugh. In the way he sees the world with big, innocent eyes. His existence brings me enough happiness for a lifetime. Although my struggles are different than they were a decade or two ago, there are still moments in my life that take a toll on my mental state of mind. Even so, I remember the miracle of life in the tiny body I helped create. Among the fog that clouds my happiness from time to time, I remember the intelligence of my little boy and how he is growing into his own person. Soon he will find his own vision, he will define what happiness means to him, and I will be the director in *his* life as my parents and friends were in mine.

With all the adversaries, injustice, and struggles in life, it is still full of joy. No matter what you do or where you are, always keep your spirit high, dream far, see life beyond imagination and never lose hope.

Reflection Activity

1. If your life was one color, what color would it be and why?

_____

_____

_____

_____

_____

_____

_____

_____

_____

2. What is life without color?

_____

_____

_____

_____

_____

_____

_____

_____

3. Why do we need color in our lives? And why is it so important to have?

_____

_____

_____

_____

_____

_____

_____

_____

_____

4. What are the values in your life?

_____

_____

_____

_____

_____

_____

_____

_____

5. If you got the chance to build your own family, what type of relationship would you create with your partner and children?

_____

_____

_____

_____

_____

_____

_____

_____

_____

6. What is one small thing in your daily life that brings you
   happiness?

_____

_____

_____

_____

_____

_____

_____

7. What does happiness mean to you?

_____

_____

_____

_____

_____

_____

_____

_____

_____

Your life will be colorful if you begin adding color to it!
It is your own decisions that will determine the outcome of your life
- Let the grays of the world seep with color and fold yourself into
the comfort of knowing that life is a coloring book only you can fill
out.

PART THREE

Strive and Take Off

courage

Chapter 1
Resilience and Aspiration

*T*here are millions of people in the world who face the darkest moments of their life every day. Even when the future looks bleak and hopeless, they *choose* to make the courageous decision to live for a better tomorrow. These people struggle for a great portion of their life, searching for comfort, peace and their own sliver of happiness, but more often than not, they are met with a despair most of us cannot even imagine.

Suffering is an inevitable human condition. While there are different volumes to suffering, there will undoubtedly come a time in your life when you will lose hope and the future will seem meaningless. This feeling of despair and hopelessness isn't something that you can just resist and ignore — it is a feeling that seizes your entire being. We cannot find happiness when darkness clouds our mind, however, you do have the power to conquer and control your feelings. Even if the suffering feels like it is unbearable, you are stronger than you believe.

Those who suffer the most are the ones with the greatest courage and the biggest hearts. Despite the suffering they have endured, they are the ones to offer you a helping hand first. They are the ones to give when all they have is nothing.

Today is not the end of the world. Tomorrow you will look back on yesterday and realize that the paralyzing feeling of suffering was something you strove to overcome with your own two hands. You pulled yourself out of the deepest depths of darkness and started on a path to a brighter future. Life is worth fighting for, there is no doubt about it. Remember all those directors in your life that helped you follow your vision. Think about those who birthed you and gave you life. Remember your family and friends who gave you hope when you needed the encouragement to move forward.

You are not the only one in the world suffering, but you are the only one who can pull yourself out of the darkness. Unlike those who struggle every day for a better life and give up trying to find one, *you* have the power to make a difference in your life. The suffering and the struggle are all a part of the process of living and attaining a better life. If you have the courage to face your fears and your darkness, you have the courage to build a future so bright that the darkness cannot penetrate it.

Fear should not be the thing that paralyzes you; it should be what motivates you. Fear is something we all share. Together, it keeps us united and stronger.

Rejoice over the life you were given and the people you've met. Your life is a blessing, you are in a place where you can feel safe, secure, and in a stable community where law and order was built to protect you. You can speak out, defend your ideas, and freely give your opinions. You don't have to worry about someone randomly walking up to you with a gun pointed at your head for sharing your ideas and faith, you don't have to worry about a bomb being dropped when you're playing with your kids outside or riding your bicycle down the street. You have fresh air, clean water, clothes on your back and a roof over your head. Tomorrow is another day and the struggles we face today only make the promise of tomorrow even sweeter.

There is a reason we were given the life we have. All the struggles, hardship, happiness, vision, and hope that occurs in our life has happened for a reason. We must not take for granted the life we were given because when we do, all the hard work we've put in our lives up until now would have been for naught. If you find that your routine in life has normalized into something you loathe, instead of making a rash decision, take a moment to breathe. Breathe and then make a change. Change your routine, quit your job, take a chance and make a new normal for your life because every day should bring you excitement.

"The greatest glory in living lies, not in never falling, but rising every time we fall."

-Nelson Mandela

Have the courage to look beyond trivial matters and into the future where you can thrive. The truth of the matter is, there is nothing normal about the lives we live. Society tells us that we need to grow up learning and taking extracurriculars, aspire towards higher education, graduate, get a job, a house, start a family and support that family until you grow old, retire, and then die. This is the "standard" routine of life that many of us in comfort are told to do. But our lives were made for something so much bigger than what we *should* do.

When people get married, they "tie a knot" together for an eternity, but when we are born, what is it that we are supposed to do? There is nothing tying us down to one thing in life. The trivial matters that we ponder every day may not have any meaning in the grand specter of things. Everyone is only doing what they *think* they need to do to have a fulfilling life. No one tells us what we need to do to be happy or how we muster up courage when our future looks dark.

All we know is what society tells us.

Living a comfortable life, witnessing the injustice going on in the Middle East, in Africa, in South America, in Southeast Asia - - in all parts of the world that has yet to fall into a brainwashing "societal norm," we think that this is normal. The problem is bigger than us, there is nothing we can do about it, there will always be bad things happening in the world, violence, poverty, hunger, injustice, we grow up learning that these things can never be changed because it has existed for too long.

But life is anything but normal and we all need to remember that the suffering we face is a reason to have courage and move forward. Life is a challenge and while it might not all be fair; we need to remember that there isn't just one path in life. There isn't a "right" way to live life. The struggles and dreams we have been uniquely our own. No one can take that away from us. What we do with what we are given in life is entirely up to us. Give up or strive forward? It is up to us to decide, but keep in mind that our life is full of colors, so unique to who we are and what we've made of it.

If the world seems dark, focus on the small moments of happiness in your day. Hold onto the remnants of your dreams and fight your way to a bigger and brighter future.

Back in 1980, when I was still a child and my family had to flee Afghanistan due to the turmoil accumulating, we returned to Iran. Everything my family had, the big house, security, dogs, maids, everything my parents worked towards and saved for the last several years was gone in an instant.

From 1979-1980, the Islamic revolution ended the Pahlavi Dynasty, which had lasted for over 4 decades. Like Afghanistan, Iran was going through some major changes both politically and socially. Many officials and heads of major entities were replaced, their position taken from them and given no compensation in return. Similarly, many distinguished people, highly educated, renowned personalities, members of the royal family and their affiliates, as well as diplomats began to flee Iran.

Despite all the change occurring, my father was obligated to return to Iran - and so he did. Though he could have fled like many were doing, he had made the unfortunate mistake of following where his duty had called. By doing so, the path of our family's future went down a path that would take years, if not decade, to stabilize. We could have fled to the US or UK like many of his colleagues at the embassy but returning to Iran set in motion horrifying and life-threatening events that I was too young to do anything about.

During the process of moving back, there were some complications we had faced, and my father decided to delay his return to Iran to deal with these complications, while my mother, younger brother, and I flew back to a home I barely remembered. We returned with very little of our belongings. Since my father had to stay a few more months in Kabul, he decided to bring the rest of our belongings that we had accumulated in our time in Afghanistan and other countries with him by a large moving truck. He had planned to rent a truck, hire a driver, and come back to Iran with another colleague.

When we returned without my father, our whole life was swept up in a whirlwind of uncertainty. Upon our arrival, airport security and revolutionary guards confiscated our passports and never returned them. Our life was thrown into chaos no one expected. Among all the changes going on, we didn't know what would happen to my father or our family. Many people around us who stayed in Iran and were highly ranked in the military, those in foreign affairs, and other government positions were arrested and persecuted. It was a distressing time without any stability. After living through the various coups in Afghanistan and then coming home to the turmoil in Iran, it seemed as if the suffering of my family would never end.

My family and I waited for my father to return. After staying in Kabul for a few months, coming back to Iran with the truck and his colleague was only supposed to take about a week or a few days more, but instead it took them almost a month to reach Iran. My mother, brother, and I worried every day for my father's safety. We had no idea what had happened or why it was taking him so long to return. Amidst the change in Iran and the chaos in Afghanistan, the worst possible outcome haunted our thoughts.

When my father finally did return home, our belongings from the last several years were gone. Everything was gone. My father was safe, but what he had endured to get back home was traumatic. On his way to Iran, he had been taken hostage by the Soviet Union patrol and had somehow, miraculously escaped.

However, once he was free from the Soviet Union, a couple days later he was then taken by the freedom fighters, Mujaheddin. His journey home was the beginning of the struggle and hardship that we would have to face as a family after returning to Iran.

I will never forget the day when the 20ft container truck pulled up to the front of our house in Tehran. It was a day my family never thought would come, we had begun to think that the worst had happened. Before my father's return, my mother had contacted some connections we had in Afghanistan to see where he was, but no one knew. We waited for his return for days, if not weeks. It wasn't until one of my father's old colleagues based in Iran told us that my father had been taken hostage by the Soviet Union and the Freedom Fighters. He said that the story was on BBC news and written about in the Guardian. In the following days after the news, I could see the suffering my mother was going through, thinking that the father of her children was dead.

However, one day I heard my father's voice call out to us, telling us to open the door. I was in disbelief and delighted. We had all thought that my father had died and that he had vanished without a trace. I felt a fierce joy and the release of relief as my brother and I ran outside, welcoming him with a big hug. It was one of the happiest moments of my life. Seeing a father, we had all thought was dead was the epitome of my happiness. However, shortly after our brief reunion, we noticed all the bullet holes piercing the side of the truck. There was barely any part that wasn't unscathed. It could have been my father. While it must have been so frightening for my parents, as a young kid, it looked amazing and unbelievable.

It was over the course of a few weeks that my father had endured life threatening events and succumbed to thieves and smugglers that stole our livelihood. Though our stuff was gone, and the truck had endured quite the hardship, we were lucky that my father returned to us in one piece. I think back to the bullet holes that had impaled the truck, and how easily that truck could have been my father. If he would have died out there, we would have never known. We would keep waiting for his return, never truly knowing his fate. The fact that he came back to us alive was a miracle in itself.

However, despite all of us being together, our suffering was far from over. The first three to four years after our return to Iran was extremely difficult. Though the new government had called upon all deployed diplomats back to the country, we weren't in the good graces of the new power. My whole family had to go through various screenings, interrogations, and endless security checks. Even at the age of 10, I was also asked to go through the trauma of interrogations.

We weren't welcomed back with open arms but forced to receive punishment. My father lost his job, and my parents were not only banned from traveling overseas indefinitely but also banned from working in general. The government took everything that belonged to us; they seized our land and equities. We no longer lived a comfortable life as a diplomatic family, living in luxury abroad. We now had nothing. Every day was a struggle, and I could see my parents fighting to build a life from nothing. We had gone through so much hardship over the years and rebuilding a life was another challenge we had to have the courage to overcome.

Despite the struggle we endured, we were certainly not the only ones facing such grievances. In northern Iran, I had two uncles and two aunts, along with a handful of cousins. One of my uncles had just built a new house and they all lived next to each other.

However, during the transition in Iran, chaos broke out. Some of Baha'i houses were burned to the ground and others were broken into and totally destroyed by some local hardliners. My aunts and uncles were victims of such violence and attacks. They were lucky to escape with their lives.

Many of my cousins, aunts, and uncles escaped their burning houses and fled from those wanting to kill them. With all of their belongings and livelihood in ashes, many of them ran away barefoot, trying to look for shelter and safety. There were some locals willing to take them in, hiding them and giving them shelter until it was safe for them to flee. A couple of my cousins even hid inside of a fridge for some time as they ran from the local hardliners that were intent on killing them. After the revolution, the changes happening within the country were larger than the government itself. Many Baha'is faced hatred and violence because of their beliefs. It was a period of agony and sorrow as Baha'i livelihoods were ripped away.

It would have been easy to give up. We had nothing anyways, so there would be nothing to lose by quitting, but in spite of everything, we fought for a better tomorrow. Piece by piece, we started to rebuild our life. We slowly built our home again, getting a fridge, stove, table, seat, fan, heater, food, and other necessities. These were small victories we focused on. Reattaining these items were our small slices of happiness that gave us hope and made us brave enough to live another day.

To this day, when I think back to everything that happened in my childhood, I wonder how life under those challenging situations could be bearable. Now that I am older, living in a safe country, and able to talk with my parents every day, I marvel at the strength my family and I had in the past. We had rebuilt a life in

Iran, and though it wasn't much, it was something. With our own two hands, we put the pieces of our lives back together and didn't just stop when we were comfortable, but we challenged ourselves to live a better future.

Living in Japan now, surrounded by so many good people, but despite their best intentions, they don't always realize what it is like to endure the suffering of trying to *merely* survive. It isn't only Japan, but in many parts of the world it is hard for us to truly understand what it means to survive due to the security and privilege we have every day. Suffering has so many layers to it, and one doesn't triumph over the others. Even in a safe country like Japan, many people have lost their loved ones due to natural disasters, illness, suicide, but outside of these incidences, there is security. Understanding the feeling of searching for a single piece of bread so that our family won't go hungry isn't something that we can all grasp.

The safety we are born into or that we have secured for ourselves is something that prohibits us from understanding the struggle of survival. Perhaps we struggle with bills or our relationships, or day-to-day problems we encounter, but most of us have access to clean water and have the means to eat a filling meal. Suffering to such an extent is an experience no one should have to go through, but even so, because we don't recognize the struggle to survive on a day-to-day basis, we end up not being able to *truly* appreciate the value of what our parents and grandparents had to endure to build the life they have today.

Everyone's suffering is different and takes on many different forms, but when I look at the life, I have built for myself and the past that I endured, I cannot explain the gratitude and pride I feel for being able to have the courage to push forward. Not just gratitude and pride for myself, but for those in my life that have helped me become the person I am today. I learned so much from the chaos in my childhood. I learned from the struggle and resilience I'd endured, but I also learned by witnessing how my parents acted in the difficult situation they were forced into.

I am truly fortunate to have such strong parents filled with courage and faith in a brighter future. I am so proud of them and grateful for all that they have given me in a time when it was hard to see beyond the suffering. This period in my life made me strong enough to build a life and strive in Canada all by myself. I cannot plan when suffering is going to happen nor can I expect a normal and ideal life, but what I can do is act. When darkness clouds my days, I've learned that accepting what is happening and *doing* something about it. This is the best way to strive for a better future.

In the summer of 2003, I traveled to an Afghan refugee camp where I was working on my research and writing my doctorate dissertation on security for my studies at the University of Cambridge. During my visit at this particular refugee camp, I came across a man by the name of Salman. I wasn't a stranger to refugee camps, I had spent a portion of my life living in one and I'd come across many people who had suffered and searched for a better life, but meeting Salman and hearing his story, something inside me changed. I felt as if I had learned something so innately human through hearing his story.

For two months, I worked on my research and was able to visit a few Afghan and Iraqi refugee camps. It had been almost two decades since I last visited Iran, and I prepared and obtained all the necessary documentation and clearances that I needed from the

Iranian government and the UNHCR (United Nations High Commissioner for Refugees). During my research trips, Iran hosted the largest refugee population in the world. Over 3 million Afghans and Iraqis were seeking shelter in refugee camps along the border.

Afghan and Iraqi Refugee camps border of Iran - 2003/2004

After the Taliban attack on the U.S. in September of 2001, the U.S. launched airstrikes to overthrow the Taliban in Afghanistan. As a result, over 3 million Afghan civilians fled to neighboring countries, such as Iran or Pakistan. The flood of refugees forced Iran to provide them shelter throughout the borders. Though Afghanistan has had a long history with turmoil, violence, and displacement, this was one of the most troubling incidents.

Once I received the clearance, I needed along with the UNHCR and the Ministry of Interior's supervision, I was able to visit and spend a few days among the many refugees, hearing their voices and gathering information to complete my research.

However, what I found among the border refugee camps was far more heart wrenching than I could have ever imagined.

We search all of our lives for the meaning of existence. We follow faith because that guides us to an answer, we dig into our ancestry or into history to try to find meaning, but life and our existence isn't an easy thing to answer simply. For some reason or another, life isn't always fair and just. There are things in our lives that we cannot control and sometimes we will never know why bad things happen to good people or why happiness is so hard to find. Life is a mystery that we put meaning into. The people who color our lives and give us hope, they help us add meaning to our lives and give us something to live for. But what if these people no longer existed? What if our hope in life is our children or our loved ones? Are they the end goal of our vision? If that is the case, what is our life once they are gone?

There is a significant difference between being human and human being.

Among the hundreds of refugees, I met and talked with, I came to realize the extreme hardship and life-threatening moments they faced. Many had suffered even worse than I had endured, yet I sympathized with their stories, knowing how desperately they all wanted to have a better life, a life of comfort and happiness instead of suffering and pain.

It was then when I came across Salman. He was a middle-aged Afghan in his 40's. He told me that he was a father of 5 who lived in a small town near the main city, Ghandehar, with his children, his wife, his mother, younger brother, and sister. When I asked what had happened and why he was at the camp, the story he told me was darker and more painful than anything I could have ever imagined.

Salman had told me that he started his morning as usual. He left home, as he did each morning, with a bag full of handmade items he sold at the nearby market. Once he had sold his wares, he would buy food from the market on his way home as he always did. However, that day was different. He had set his handcrafted items on the floor along with other hard-working locals trying to make a profit in order to feed their families when he heard a loud explosion. The U.S. airstrike had dropped a bomb near their town that was supposed to hit militant facilities.

Salman rushed home as fast as he could once, he heard the explosion, but it was too late. The bomb had mistakenly landed on civilian property. His humble, muddy home was decimated. There was nothing left of his home. All five of his children had died. His wife was dead, his siblings were dead, and his mother had died. In a blink of an eye, his whole family was gone. Everything he worked hard for, every bit of hope he had entrusted to his children, the better life he wanted for all of them, everything was gone.

When I heard his story, I was at a loss for words. He had lost 9 members of his family that day. Salman had lost everything. Everything he was and everything he dreamed was taken from him by a mistargeted missile. I could not imagine the pain and suffering I was hearing. The unthinkable sorrow and agony he must have gone through. No one should have to suffer so terribly, the world was unfair, and yet Salman was alive to tell his story.

I asked him how he could even go on. How could he stand up and not give up even though everyone he loved had died? I asked him what made him continue living life with all the agony and nothing to fight for?

"Courage, my brother, courage"

His eyes bore into mine, so transparent and vulnerable, but I could see the strength in his eyes and the warmth of his heart. He held my hands as he told me that *courage* was the only thing keeping him going. He had the power of hope and the courage to live another day. With all the suffering, injustice, and cruelty he faced, Salman was able to pick up the pieces of his life and *try* to rebuild his life.

Since that day, I have always thought about how he survived and if he is still alive, fighting each second, he is on earth, continuing to live with the memories of his lost loved ones. Having the courage to live on must not have been easy. Seeing the bodies of his family and the destruction of his home must have been an irrevocable pain that could never be healed. Even so, Salman lived tomorrow knowing that the suffering and darkness would follow him throughout life. He knew that happiness would be harder to achieve because his loss was so deep, but still, he had the courage to live on.

I take the story of Salman with me wherever I go. His words and his story give me hope and encourages me to be brave. Knowing every day that I have lived, and I've carried around the memories of my loved ones, there is no chance I would end my life. Even if I were to lose everything dearest to me, I have to think about Salman who had the courage to simply *live*. There is meaning in life and why we should make the conscious decision to stay alive and strive. I think about my child who has kept me alive with his existence, joy, and the beautiful memories we create together. I need to be strong and continue living, so that I don't fail him. Our life is our own, it is what we make of it. It is colored by our experiences and people in our life. It has meaning and to think of that lightly is doing an injustice to all you care for and all that cares for you.

In the summer of 2004, I went back to the refugee camps to complete my writing. I looked for Salman when I returned, but unfortunately there were no signs of him. Despite asking and trying, no one knew how to contact him or how to find him. To this day, I wonder where Salman is now. Is he alive? Is he using his hope and courage to build a new life? What would have happened if he didn't go through such pain and loss? There are so many questions I still have that I may never find the answer to. However, despite not being able to find him or see how he is doing, I believe in the hope and courage he has.

I am and will always be grateful for the story he shared with me. It is an experience I would never wish on my worst enemy, but it has opened up my eyes to the world. I wake up every morning reminding myself how privileged I am to have the life I do, blessed with parents, a loving family, and amazing friends. I am in a safe environment where I can be happy and chase my dreams. I am lucky to be alive.

On the other hand, I also remind myself that life isn't always beautiful. For thousands upon thousands of years, inequality and cruelty has also existed. Our lives will always be filled with obstacles trying to tear us down.

Suffering is a human condition none of us can escape. The confines of societal pressures will also be there holding us back. There are so many obstacles in life, but we must have courage and aspiration to boost the meaning and value of our life. We must fight for the future and the next generations.

It isn't always easy to be resilient and aspire to something greater. If it were easy, then we would never grow as individuals. However, seeing the extraordinary power of hope combined with a strong sense of courage from Salman, I realized that these two attributes complement each other when we need them the most. As long as we can strive towards having hope and courage, then we can aspire to be resilient no matter the obstacles we face. We need to be strong and honor our lives with hope and courage so that we will come out on top when we face our darkest troubles.

Be fair in thy judgment and guarded in thy speech. Be unjust to no man and show all meekness to all men. Be as a lamp unto them that walk in darkness, a joy to the sorrowful, a sea for the thirsty, a haven for the distressed, an upholder and defender of the victim of oppression

-Baha'u'llah

Resilience and Aspiration

Chapter 2
Perilous Journey

Courage is the reassurance of hope. It accompanies and inspires your goals and plans so that you might go forth into the future more prepared.

Throughout history, men and women fought to gain their freedom, moving between nations in hopes for a better life. Those who succeeded were sometimes seen as symbols of aspiration. They were living a dream others could only aspire towards.

Millions of people have lost their lives or lost their loved ones to unjust warfare and the chaos of an unruly state without rhyme or reason. There have been so many innocent lives lost because arrogant leaders put their desires above the lives of citizens. There have been many wars that have ended in vain and went on in meaningless turmoil for years. There is no winner in a war where so much blood has been shed and so many lives sacrificed -- especially not when nothing was gained in the end. There are only losers left standing in the rubble.

"The world will not be destroyed by those who do evil, but by those who watch them without doing anything."

-Albert Einstein

In such wars, very few people consider the lives of those occupying the areas that act as a battlefield. There is rarely any warning given to the people whose lives become uprooted as turmoil and chaos disrupt their daily life. What would you do if you woke up tomorrow only to see your local government in chaos and disarray? What would you do if bombs were dropped near your town, if fighter jets streamed overhead as you made your morning coffee, or if the street you lived on erupted in violence? When your hopes and dreams blow to pieces before your very eyes, how would you react?

According to the 1951 Refugee Convention, "[a refugee is] a person who is outside his/her country of nationality or habitual residence; has a well-founded fear of persecution because of his/her race, religion, nationality, membership in a particular social group or political opinion; and is unable or unwilling to avail himself/herself of the protection of that country, or to return there, for fear of persecution." This definition of refugee by UNHCR explicitly states that refugees are people who have fled war, violence, conflict or persecution and have crossed an international border to find safety in another country. It is more often than not that these people flee with little more than the clothes on their back, leaving behind homes, possessions, jobs and loved ones.

Being a refugee was the most important phase in my life. It was difficult, tiring, and there were times I began to falter, but I had the courage to stand up again. It was a struggle that I *needed* to experience in order to get to where I am today. I learned so much during my time as a refugee, and when I look back to that time in my life, I am still in shock at the life I had back then. I was surrounded by difficult times, friends who have lost loved ones as I had, and somehow, I managed to keep my spirits high and have the courage to move forward. I didn't give up dreaming for a better future.

However, my journey in *becoming* a refugee had hardened me before I got to the camp. It had scared me and broken me in ways that I had never imagined. It was early July 1985 and summer in the middle of the desert was stifling and unbearable.

After saying goodbye to my family and leaving behind all my friends and relatives, I was accompanied by my father from Tehran to Khash, a city in the southeast part of Iran and about 200 km from the border of Pakistan. I said my final goodbye to my father in that city, not knowing if this would be the last time, I would see him again. After leaving him, I met the other five compatriots that would join me on the journey to the refugee camp. Among the five, three were my cousins who had also suffered hardship and persecution because of their faith.

Together, we began our journey, escorted by two paid smugglers. The atmosphere was tense among our group. We were all scared of what could happen and though I had my cousins by my side, no one knew if we could trust the smugglers. Our lives were in their hands, and we were given no other option but to trust that they would bring us to the refugee camp.

The first instructions from the smugglers were to lay flat in the back of a truck as we drove out of the city. We did so without any sense of direction as to where we were heading. Time seemed to go on forever, but after driving about 30 minutes, the smugglers had stopped the truck and told us to get out. We were in the middle of the desert with only the promise that the smugglers would return at dusk with camels, food, and water.

We had not seen where we were going, nor did we know where we were at. All around us were beige deserts and beige mountains. All we knew was that we were headed to Pakistan, but where the border was, none of us could say. The fear and anxiety the smugglers left us in was overwhelming and waiting for dusk seemed endless. We were all young, from 16 to 28, and I was the youngest of the group. Despite our age, we were all scared. Six young boys standing in the middle of the desert with nowhere to go and only the promise of smugglers we didn't know if we could trust.

After hours of waiting, the smugglers finally returned right after sunset, as promised with the camels. However, the food and water they promised would sustain us on the trip was nowhere to be seen. They gave us nothing but bread, which was hard as a rock and too old to eat without breaking teeth. As much as we wanted to complain about what we were given, we couldn't. Our lives were in their hands, and we had heard that some people who tried to pass through the borders with smugglers were robbed, tortured, raped or killed. There was truly nothing we could do except take what they offered us and hope that we got through the border in one piece.

We had to wait until nightfall before we could begin our journey. Under the security of the darkness, we had each been given a camel that knew the dangerous terrain well. It was impossible to see anything while we rode at night, I could barely see the camel's head as I rode on top of him. The terrain was horrendous, covered with sand and hard rocks, but luckily the camels knew where to go and how to navigate the darkness.

Our journey took seven days and six nights. During daylight, we would travel on foot, resting from time to time, but by nightfall, we rode our camels. The journey wasn't easy, and before this, I had never ridden a camel in my lifetime, nor was I used to having to stay awake all night. It was very difficult to keep my eyes open for hours on end while riding on top of a camel in the dead of night. There was even a time when one of my cousins had fallen asleep one night and fell off of his camel. He was lucky that there were no sharp rocks where he fell and that he was able to come away uninjured.

After the first couple of days on our journey, I began to grow more anxious. It didn't help how untamed the terrain and desert were in July. The heat was getting to all of us. Not only did the sun beat ruthlessly down on us, but the ground below us soaked in the heat and radiated it back to us. It was as if we were locked in a sauna with nothing to reprieve us of the stifling heat.

The long nights and hot days were wearing on me and I didn't know where the border was, nor did I know when we would pass through it. According to the stories we heard from former refugees who passed through the Pakistan borders, as well as from our smugglers, the border was highly guarded by many soldiers and patrols that constantly made their rounds.

The Iranian government and border guards knew that there would be many people who would try to be smuggled out or try to flee the country. As a result, detail on the border was a high priority for the government. Keeping the border clean and closed was a major task that the government worked hard on imposing. Tracking down all who tried to pass through, arresting the smugglers and those who tried to flee, and bringing them back to the government for "justice." Of course, justice and justification were all double standard and only relevant to what the new government saw fit. When there is oppression, persecution, and injustice, people begin seeking and fleeing to a safer place. There would be no reason for people to leave their home and go through such hardship otherwise. However, the government didn't see it that way.

After the second day of our journey, we were all dying for a drop of water and food to eat. Though they had promised my father and their other employers that we would all get enough food and drink, the smugglers later told us that there was no water to drink. Walking on foot through the desert during the hottest season of the year, the temperature was no less than 40 degrees Celsius and the unbearable heat seemed impossible without water. The smugglers had also brought no food, either. Each of us only had one small bag that carried our basic needs, but none of us had brought food. Before embarking on the perilous journey, we were told not to bring any food or water since the smuggler would provide enough for the whole trip.

Yet here we were, the second day of the trip and we were without food and water. We couldn't think straight, and we were all afraid of disobeying the smugglers since our lives were in their hands. How absurd and painful it was that none of us thought to carry a piece of bread, snacks, a bottle of water, a protein bar, or anything that could keep us alive. We weren't even halfway done with our journey and already we were struck with fear that prevented us from looking ahead and being more prepared.

My mind was a jumble of thoughts, torn between the agony of being away from my home and the idea that I might die on this trip. I thought of my family, my father who had told me to call him as soon as I arrived anywhere that I might have access to a phone so that he would know that all six of us were safe. I wonder if we would survive long enough for me to make that call. I thought of my 4-year-old little sister and my younger brother, who was my best buddy and whom I shared so much joy and memories with. How could we all survive? Would we survive? Would there ever be a chance to see my loved ones again?

The pain of missing them and the permanency of fleeing my home hit me after a couple of days. With no food or water, I thought more about my family and surviving this trip. I didn't know how many more days we would have to survive with nothing to sustain our energy or bodies. I didn't know when we would arrive at the next town and when we asked the smugglers about our schedule, their response was always the same: "Soon" or "Look over there. We will arrive right after crossing that mountain." We had no choice but to believe and keep quiet.

The only thing that kept us alive for another 6 days without any water was the hope in their responses. Soon. We would get there *soon*, right after those mountains. Those mountains were the goal and we all held onto that goal for life. In the grand spectrum of things, the hope of *soon* was a lie, but it was a lie that kept us alive. We wanted to believe them, so we did. If they had told us the truth, I don't think the other five or I would have been able to handle the reality of our situation.

The smugglers knew the path better than anyone, and they knew that our mettle would diminish if they told us the journey would take us over a week without any previsions. So instead, they fed us false hope in order to boost our motivation and keep us going without food and water. Losing courage and hope would have been the worst thing to happen to any of us on the journey.

If we lost hope, we wouldn't have the energy or courage to continue on.

I held onto the smuggler's words, thinking that we would soon arrive at our location. Sometimes I thought about our journey and going into Pakistan. The country we were fleeing into had their own problems and areas of need. The country was not stable, nor was it safe or clean. They had their own issues with poverty and the risk it took to get there was grave. We had no one but ourselves and the hopes our parents had for our well-being and happiness.

However, one thing Pakistan did have was a sliver of security we wouldn't be able to get back home. We were given the opportunity to start our lives over and attain the basic rights that we were starved of in our own country. Going to Pakistan meant hope for our future. It would be the magic fix we all longed for, but it was the transition we all needed.

We wouldn't find our future here, but it was a terminal where we would wait for the train to our future to arrive. It provided us the possibility to continue our education, secure work, and build a life we couldn't in Iran because we were Baha'i. We all had so much hope and were determined to make our parents and our culture proud of what we could do after settling in a new country. We just needed to be brave and have courage on our journey.

We continued our perilous passage and by the third and fourth day, we were all extremely dehydrated and close to dying under the relentless heat of the summer. Without a single drop of water, it seemed impossible to carry on. The desert was endless, and the mountains appeared to be an impossible distance away. We didn't know if we would live to see the day where we could finally gulp down a cool glass of water. However, on the fifth day of our journey, one of the smugglers mentioned that we could change our path slightly in order to go by a "nice lake" that was 30 to 40 kilometers away.

The hope the word *soon* had on us began to grow more promising as we changed course in order to reach the lake. I would never forget the moment each of us raised to our feet, more determined than we felt all week, and began walking. It was a do or die situation and we began to feel the energy of being alive once again. We could see our future once again, we just had to make it to the lake.

By the time we reached the lake, it was dark, and we had been riding our camels for a few hours. One of the smugglers called to us, saying that the lake was here, but we couldn't see it in the moonlight. There was no reflection from the moonlight as we had thought, and it took a while for us to realize that the "lake" was right in front of us. It was barely big enough to even be called a pond. It was nothing more than a body of water that was two diameters by two diameters and the substance was filled with so many insects and other bugs. Thankfully the darkness obscured the color of the water as well, because despite whatever was floating in the water, our thirst overtook us.

We reached down and all began to drink to our heart's content, not caring what disease or filth coated the water. We were just relieved to be taking in some sort of liquid, it didn't matter how clean it was. I was so distracted by the relief of water that it took me a moment to realize that the camels, too, reached their heads down towards the small pond and we drank side by side. This was and felt like the water from the heavens. The water could not have come at a better time. It had rejuvenated us and fulfilled the small hope we had. It gave us the courage and bravery to carry on and to fight another day.

To this day, I will never forget the value of water and life. We didn't think or worry about the quality of the water. We didn't give another thought to the infections or sickness we might befall because of the dirty pool of water. We simply drank in order to live. Life found a way and we continued on our journey for another couple of days. Though we had drunk our fill of water on the fifth day, we went without food and water for a couple more days until we reached the border.

Under the guided advice of our smugglers, we said goodbye to the camels and snuck into a small truck that was waiting for us right before sunrise. We hid in the back of the truck and covered ourselves with large sheets. It was a half day drive before we reached a small village that the smugglers had a stronghold in and connections with locals. We had successfully gotten through the border. The future looked promising and after the treacherous journey, the smugglers had brought us closer to our destination.

Despite getting through, however, we would still have to pass through three of the major patrol stands in Pakistan before reaching Quetta. The smugglers told us that each vehicle would be stopped and asked to provide an ID before continuing. Though we were no longer in the country that oppressed us, we still needed to reach the UNHCR in Quetta, about 900 kilometers away from where we were on the Iran-Pakistan border. If we were found out, the Pakistan government and guards could easily send us back to Iran once they discovered we had been smuggled out. Until we reached UNHCR and received our refugee ID cards, our lives were still in jeopardy. We were not protected yet and still needed to practice caution if we were going to make it to our destination alive.

Even so, we were happy to have made it over the border. One small milestone was reached, and we celebrated our small victory before focusing on the next perilous milestones. Shortly after our arrival to the small village, the smugglers took us to a place where we could eat and drink. I drank 6 large glasses of water and 5 full bottles of soda. We were saved and utterly thankful that we were able to reach a safer place where we had access to food and water. For a whole hour, we gorged ourselves on the deliciousness of food and the satisfaction of water before our journey in Pakistan began.

When we began the second half of our perilous journey, we filed into a small minibus accompanied by 5 - 10 locals. The ride took us over 10 hours and we embarked at sunset, driving throughout the night and into the early morning. There were people sitting on the roof of the minibus as well as inside. Two of the refugees that fled with me sat on the roof while another two sat inside of the cabin, covering their faces and hiding every time we got close to a parole station.

One of my cousins and I were sitting in the front of the minibus next to the driver. Our faces were covered with a veil and makeup. We were to act as women since the guards hesitated to speak and check inside when there was a female passenger in the vehicle. The driver instructed us to keep our heads down and act shy and hesitant if the guard should try talking to us. I was nervous and my heart was beating so loud, but I needed to keep it under control. These patrol checks were life or death moments, not just for me, but for the others of us as well.

I had just turned 16 and before fleeing to become a refugee, I had never been away from my parents, nor had I faced such challenges and hardships on my own. None of what we were going through was "normal." There was no constructive plan or preparation in place to keep us alive and secure. We felt as if our parents' prayers kept us safe and that God was watching us through all the hardship we faced and the life-threatening incidents we survived.

After hours of driving and going through checkpoint after checkpoint, we finally passed through all the patrol stations unscathed and reached Quetta city. Upon our arrival, we were quickly directed to a motel where we could rest and prepare ourselves for the next morning where we would have to present our case and request for asylum to the UNHCR office.

An asylum seeker is someone who is seeking international protection but whose claim for refugee status has not yet been determined. In contrast, a refugee is someone who has been recognized under the 1951 Convention relating to the status of refugees to be a refugee '. Amnesty International (www.amnesty.org/)

We were extremely exhausted. Everything that had happened up until now was surreal. We sat in a motel, on a bed, waiting to receive our documents from the UNHCR after we had presented our case. I was finally in a place where I would be safe for a couple of days, but somehow, it didn't feel real. After waiting a few days at the motel, we were given train tickets and a few other documents and information for the third and final stretch of our trip. We were supposed to head to Lahore where most Baha'is were being taken as refugees.

The train ride was going to be an 18-hour ride, stopping in many places in between. Luckily, the few days we stayed in the motel in Quetta city was a massive relief and relaxation that we needed. After a little more than a week of always looking over our shoulder, wondering if we would be safe, if we would make it to Pakistan or to the UNHCR office, the journey had finally paid off. Those few days at the motel had refreshed our mental state and boosted our courage. We began to realize how well we did in the trials we faced so far. My journey to becoming a refugee made me realize that the world is not a safe place, and the best we can do is to protect ourselves and be prepared for whatever might come our way.

After a few days soaking up well needed rest at a motel in Quetta city, we receive our train tickets from someone who knew the route to the refugee camp and had dealt with many Baha'i asylum seekers before, we were told to be incredibly careful and not to come out of the cabin when the train stopped. There would still be guards and patrols that were looking for anyone who had illegally entered Pakistan. The gentleman also advised us to try to bribe the guards or police in the worst-case scenario. If they found out our situation and our lives were in danger, this was the best option because many of the guards were quite flexible when cash was offered. Although it might seem scandalous for the guards to take bribes, we understood that these people came from a very low-income environment, and they also had to face an unfair society that we could not see.

After being instructed by our guide, we began our last leg of our journey. The trip was supposed to be 18 hours, though this was by far the easiest part of the perilous journey. We didn't have to walk under extreme heat in the desert with no food, or hide under blankets for hours, or drive through the night, dressed like women. However, even though it was easier, it was still not without risk. On our train ride to the refugee camps, there were a couple of incidents where a few officers discovered us. Since I was the youngest and small, I followed everyone's lead, being more cooperative and holding back my opinions or complaints. The eldest member in our group dealt with the negotiating, talking, and bribing of the guards. We were lucky that they took the bribe and let us continue our journey.

The journey to the camp was longer than 18 hours. There were numerous delays on the way, but after a couple days on the train and sleeping in the cabin, we finally arrived in Lahore safely and in one piece. We were directed to a place where all newcomers stayed until our acquaintances or someone, we knew who previously entered the camp came to pick us up.

Although I only spent two years in Pakistan as a refugee, from July 1985 to February 1988, my mindset had changed so drastically during this time. My thoughts deepened and I saw the world in a whole new light; they developed within as well as without. I knew that there were people who came before me to this place or others similar, some lost their lives to the injustice that drove them to seek safety while many others moved onto someplace *different*. These people left footprints in their wake, allowing us to follow and continue on our journey.

The journey I embarked on was far from safe. I didn't wake up one day, realize the oppression happening in my country and decide to fly and take refuge in Pakistan. My journey was far more perilous than that. The trials I went through and the obstacles that I faced just to reach a safe place that might give me a chance for a better future were numerous. The life-or-death situations I was in made me realize that it isn't enough to just hope for everything to work out seamlessly, but that I needed to have the courage and strength to carry on.

To have hope is inspiring, but to share hope with courage is how you will face the dangers in the world and the unpredictable moments that will happen in your life. This courage will be what elevates you, flooding your world with colors of understanding that is filled with enlightenment. This is one of the major journeys where I realized what it means to *be* courageous. I not only saw it in the other refugees who fled with me, living every day trying to survive, but in myself. When we have courage, we have the ability to take the broken pieces of our life and try to make something better. Not every obstacle is a set-back, sometimes you need obstacles in your life to reach a more colorful future.

Perilous Journey

Chapter 3
Transition Phase - Resurrection

I can still remember the incredible people I met during my time as a refugee. They all played a distinct role in who I've become today, shaping my young adult life, teaching me what it means to be resilient and thoughtful, and reminding me every day to fight for my goal. Though they helped me become a man, the burden of the refugee camp was a heavy weight to carry as a teenager. We all lived day-by-day, never knowing how life might change in the next 24 hours. While we enjoyed the small pleasures of each day, we were anxious about the wait. Every day, we waited to hear our names come up, or to hear which embassy would give us an interview date. We waited to know which country would accept us and allow us to start a new life, away from our struggles and oppressors. We did nothing but wait and grow our patience. This was the transition period. A limbo of time that crept forward slowly.

Throughout my first year, I lived with seven other guys, some were more than 10 years older than I was. Fortunately, my two cousins - Andy and OJ were also placed in my living quarters. They were like brothers to me, and I was very blessed to have them and a few others as roommates. They had lost so much throughout their life after the revolution because of their beliefs and religion. Their house was burned to the ground and all their belongings were thrown into a well and destroyed. They weren't the only ones, however. We all suffered to a great extent, the innumerable amount of oppression and pain we experienced was something we all shared.

My roommates and other friends visiting us for lunch - Refugee 1985/86

In the course of my time with these roommates, I got to know each one of them, learning their stories and finding the value in their lives. Looking back now, I was so fortunate to grow and live with them. They taught me so many things as a young man. It was incredible to see that all of these men had faced such loss and adversities, yet they were still able to stand up on their own two feet and keep hoping and believing that there is a brighter tomorrow.

We lived in a room that was no bigger than 10 square meters, the toilet was dirty and the wall outside where we used to take a shower was nothing much to look at. Most of us could showered once a week due to the lack of water, and the water we used was a mix of boiling water along with normal water. It was quite a difficult lifestyle, especially in the winters when it was cold. But it was shelter and compared to the suffering most of us had endured back home, we were grateful for the little we had. Once a week, we would alternate who was in charge of cooking and other household chores. Since I was the youngest, I didn't need to cook, but I regularly helped wash dishes and volunteered to help buy food or clean.

During the day, there wasn't much to do. Sometimes we would hang out outside or play cards indoors. We often chatted with one another or visited other acquaintances. Usually, I would go with my cousins and hang out with their friends, playing football, volleyball, cards, and other games we came up with. Once a month, we would go to the UNHCR office and pick up our money payment. Every refugee received about 500 rupees per month, which was the equivalent of $3.00USD. It wasn't much, but it was given to us to help pay for our food, transportation and other necessities. Aside from necessary monthly payments I needed to make, I could only afford to buy a few bananas or a couple clementines each month. Other necessities such as clothes, extra food, snacks, drinks, or anything I would have had access to in Iran weren't possible.

Life was extremely difficult. Though we were in a place that was supposed to be a transition platform from our past life that was threatened by prosecution and our new life with the prospects of a better future, it was nowhere near perfect nor comfortable. We needed to be strong and stand firm. We couldn't let go of hope and we had to remind ourselves that the situation we were in wouldn't last forever. Sooner or later, we would prevail -- we had to. I needed my efforts against hardship to pay off, because if they didn't, the misery of leaving my family behind and struggling with the bare necessities that we were given would be in vain. Many of us hoped for a brighter future, yet the hardships seem innumerable.

There were a number of youth and elderly who could not take the everyday hardship of the refugee camp. After a few months, some would head back to Iran, knowing the consequences they were going to have to face there would be tougher. The government wouldn't look kindly upon their escape, but many of them thought that the consequences dealt would be shorter than their time in the camps.

Life is a struggle within itself. Sometimes, we suffer so much in these struggles that we only look for the fastest and easiest way to ease the suffering, not bothering to look at the consequences down the road. If we are faced with two evils, we are told to pick the lesser evil, but when faced with two paths of suffering, do we want to choose the path that eases our struggle the fastest or the one that has the brighter outcome? These decisions are hard, and when you have family to think about, the decisions get even more difficult.

While the paths you take in your life come from the choices you make, sometimes decisions are easier to decide when there are directors in your life that will guide you, advise you, or just listen and sympathize with you. However, if the directors in our lives aren't good or absent, we have to deal with difficult decisions on our own. And sometimes, those closest to us might not recognize the capacity of difficulties we shoulder.

Hardship is never something we wish for in life, but it makes it easier when we have someone to share it with.

We never wander down a path of suffering on our own accord, it is usually thrusted upon us in one way or another. For me, for refugees, it is oppression that drove us down the difficult path. Refugees are forced to flee their homes. Forced. Our lives were uprooted and shoved to the side. Never mind that we were living on our ancestors' holy land where our parents were born, had built their life, and where they had dreamed of growing old. Never mind the culture and heritage that ties us to the land and our homes. We were thrown out.

In spite of all the darkness, there were people around me who lit my way. They told me stories of their sacrifices and benevolence, their path in life, the loved ones they had to leave behind, and the hopes they held. Life was not simple by any means, nor was it terribly complicated either. Though the world was unjust, we just had to accept it and live with what we were given. Patience was my best companion.

"So do all who live see such times, but that is not for them to decide. All we have to decide is what to do with the time that is given to us."

-J.R.R. Tolkien, *The Fellowship of the Ring*

However, it would be a lie to say that I didn't miss home and that my life wasn't hard. While I was surrounded by so many great people, the camp wasn't home. The ultimate desire for any human being is the idea or the prospect of "home." Many people feel lost without a home, others do all they can to build or establish their own home; home is a sanctuary that many men and women throughout history fight to defend. Some people would sacrifice their lives to keep their home safe and unharmed. We see this time and time again between various nations. It is not uncommon to want to keep our livelihood unscathed from invaders.

In my second year at the refugee camp, I was lucky to have been joined by my uncle and cousins in Pakistan. Similarly, my uncle with his family had fled because of their faith as a Baha'i and their life being in danger. He lived in the northern part of Iran and when the revolution happened, he was forced to uproot his life and flee. He had just built a new house all on his own. He and his family barely settled in when local hardliners terrorized their town, destroying their property and burning the house down to ground. The adversaries that my uncle, my aunt and cousins faced were horrifying, but I was glad to have them in the camp with me.

I had a very special bond with all of them, and we were quite close back in Iran. During summer holidays, when I was living in Afghanistan and would visit Iran, I used to stay with him and his family quite often. I would play with my cousins who were a few years older than me and enjoy spending carefree time with them surrounded by the extraordinary nature of Mazandaran (Caspian Sea coast). But all of that seemed so long ago.

In Pakistan, my uncle and cousins were like my immediate family. Though they were related to me by blood, I felt a deeper connection with them that only grew at the camp. They made me feel safe and comfortable, and I was blessed to spend my last year of refugee time with them. My aunt was such a decent and lovable person. She always cared about me and cooked for me as if I were her own son. A year after I left for Canada, I heard the good news that they had also passed their interview with the Australian embassy and were given the chance to start a new life peacefully in Australia. I was grateful for all that they had given and taught me, and I was glad that they were able to build a new life someplace else.

When I was first forced to flee Iran, the number of refugees was skyrocketing with no signs of slowing down. As long as arrogant and power-hungry leaders still exist, the massive global phenomenon of displaced people will never end.

If people do not learn how to *respect* others' beliefs, lifestyles, cultures, and religions, there will always be war, and therefore, there will always be refugees. If the phenomenon of *identity* demolishes, we would not have to fight for land, race, and survival if nations began listening to each other more and appreciating the differences instead of alienating them.

Up until my days as a refugee, I had learned and slowly understood the injustices of the world. Whether from what I've experienced at school, from the coups d'état in Afghanistan, seeing the worst kind of poverty, understanding and idolizing Gandhi in India, surviving through the unrest during the revolution and the war in Iran, I learned that you could never prepare for the obstacles and hardships life threw at you. There were so many things that I learned and thought I understood.

However, after becoming a refugee, my whole world changed. Before, I was under the guidance of my parents. They supported me, protected me, helped me up when I fell down, but as a refugee, I was alone. I needed to learn how to stand on my own two feet, how to prepare myself for hardship, how to be more flexible, and have the sympathy to understand and cope with others.

In Pakistan, there were over 1,500 Baha'i refugees from all over Iran. Everyone was different, coming from different backgrounds, families, and each having their own story. Some were very heart breaking, like having a family member becoming killed or imprisoned by the government. Others spoke of the long journey they had to take just to reach Pakistan. Many of these people struggled and fought to live a life that was neither kind nor fair to them.

Being a refugee isn't easy. It wasn't easy then and it isn't easy now. All of us were forced to leave home, thinking that our lives were endangered and that a future in our home country would be nothing but abuse and oppression. We go through so much hardship and heartbreak just to land in a place where patience is our only friend, and we are forced to wait for a better future that might not even come. Being a refugee isn't only trying on your physical health, but also your mental health.

Throughout our time as refugees, we were allowed to integrate with local Pakistanis to a certain extent. However, because we were considered outsiders and refugees, we couldn't connect with them fully and we had to take measures to protect ourselves. Several fights broke out between a Baha'i refugee trying to protect their family from the harassment of local Pakistanis. Some of these fights got ugly really fast and ended up in a mess. It was a common occurrence that most of us tried to avoid. We were highly advised not to get involved in any sort of physical fight or similar behavior because of our status. The pain of being patient was unbearable at times. Some refugees were forced to be patient and calm even after a relative was stabbed to death. It was hard, but most of us endured the pain for as long as we could, but it was not uncommon for the locals to take advantage of our vulnerability and our status as a refugee.

Despite having to accept and live with all sorts of hardship, we were happy knowing that our transition was only temporary. We cherished the moments we got with new friends and though we all had darkness in our lives, we took comfort in sharing a common pain. We were like one huge family from all around Iran. We knew that there would be a better future waiting for us, we just needed to be patient. Today -- any day could be the last day we were at the camp. Our time together was limited, and once we left Pakistan, we probably would never see each other again. I treasured every day I had with the people around me. We spent so much time getting to know one another and I made numerous friends who had, hopefully, gone off to live a better life. Everyone was destined to go to a different country and live a different life. The ending was always bittersweet, but after the hardship and suffering we all faced, knowing that our friends had the opportunity to live a better life gave us hope and courage to continue our journey.

One of the fondest memories was the celebrations we would throw for a friend who was set to depart. The get together would be the night before and we would celebrate the launch of a new life. The joy and relief in their eyes were blatant and we all knew that our time would come eventually. The opportunity to live in a safer place, have access to work and an education, and given the freedom to grow and build a life was how we held onto our small lives during the refugee period in Pakistan.

Like those before me, my time to go came after two years in Pakistan. There was a deep sorrow within me. Leaving all the friends I made who've become my family was truly heartbreaking. Saying goodbye was one of the hardest things I had to do. How do you say "goodbye" and "thank you" to those who gave you courage to live on, who helped shape you both mentally and spiritually? On February 12th, 1988, I left my life as a refugee in Pakistan and flew to Canada. A whole new life was waiting for me in Canada. Though I would have no support or family or friends in Canada, it was the opportunity to start over and build a future I wouldn't be able to have in Iran.

"To live is to suffer, to survive is to find meaning in the suffering."
-Friedrich Nietzsche

Before a person can enter the refugee camp for the first time, they have to go through a phase of *Terminal Transit*, as I call it. Aspiring refugees have to wait for the UNHCR to process their documents, before receiving their official documentation and going onto the next step. After receiving documentation, the refugee has to fill forms and send a letter of request to a country they could or wish to immigrate to. In other words, if you have relatives who have already established themselves in a certain country, then you would make an application to that country's embassy. If the country recognizes your situation and your potential, you will be given an interview for that country. After the interview, you will get notified from the embassy as to whether your application has been accepted for the second interview process or if it has been denied. Being denied from a country where your family or relatives have already settled is many refugees' worst nightmare. On the other hand, if you have been accepted and passed the second interview, you'll have to go through medical check-ups before finally departing to the country you've gotten accepted into.

In the best-case scenario, this process can take up to 1 year. However, in more complicated situations, it could take 2 or more years to find placement. I was very fortunate to be accepted and embraced by one of the leading countries and the best place to live and settle into. Because I was quite young and had the potential to continue my education and contribute to the community, I was gratefully accepted into Canada.

Being a refugee hardens a person in unimaginable ways. The accumulation of suffering endured by a refugee is what makes for a brighter and more colorful future, built through the resilience of hope, and reinforced by courage. Transitioning between suffering and struggle, and peace and happiness is never easy.

Transition Phase - Resurrection

Chapter 4
Refugee and Beyond - Life from Zero

At the end of each dark tunnel, there is an even brighter future waiting. Though life is filled with brutality and injustice, hope and light will always prevail. Even if it is hard to believe that there is a brighter future waiting for you, practice patience and be ready to accept change when it comes your way. I have been through many obstacles and challenges early on in my life. Before arriving in Canada, I faced extraordinary incidences, came across indescribable experiences, and fought to survive even when darkness clouded my vision.

"It is during our darkest moments that we must focus to see the light."

-Aristotle

During my time as a refugee, I faced my suffering every day, yet it was throughout this period that I gained the most. My transition between the corrupt world my parents protected me from to an independent one where I had to face the monsters of reality on my own, had forced me to grow up and build my own character. Two years as a refugee had taught me that no matter what happened, I was in charge of my own decisions. I am the master of my own soul, and no one could change that. I was my own protector now and no family member or friend could help me with that.

Being a refugee has given me the opportunity to teach myself how to take care of myself. Though there were directors in my life who supported my vision and shed some hope onto my path, it was now up to me to create my own future. I was blessed with many kind and caring directors to watch over me as I grew up but transitioning out of childhood and into adulthood was something I needed to accomplish before moving beyond the refugee camp and into a world where I could start chasing my visions.

When starting my life in Canada, there were several major challenges that I had to face in order to survive. Though they might have seemed small, they were struggles that I had to overcome on my own. I needed to face the discomfort of being in a foreign land and instead focus on the possibilities of having a bright future ahead of me. However, being young and arriving in Canada in the middle of winter with fifteen dollars in pocket, my first impression of the country was nowhere near positive. My first season in Canada was filled with darkness and struggle.

Everyone looked and acted quite differently than me, and I was faced with culture shock and loneliness. I felt so alone and could not bear the silence I was forced to endure. My language ability prohibited me from speaking to others and as an outsider, I was hesitant to initiate conversation with strangers or try to make friends.

I had eagerly waited for months to move in and build my life here, yet upon arrival, I felt underwhelmed and overwhelmed all at once. The sudden changes were more than I could handle. I had spent two years as a refugee, dreaming of starting a new life and following my dreams, but now that I was there, it was harder to remember why I had felt so hopeful in the first place.

Coming from Pakistan where the weather and environment was warm and friendly made me feel like I had entered another universe I didn't belong in. At least in Pakistan, I was surrounded by hundreds of people and relatives whom I spent the last two years with. Despite the suffering and struggling I had to endure at the refugee camp, at least I had others to support and help me. In Canada, I felt as if I had nothing and no one. The two places couldn't have been more different.

For the first two months in Canada, my stay was horribly difficult, and I kept questioning my decision to start a life here. However, the darkest nights create the brightest stars, and suddenly, something just *clicked*. I knew, deep down, that no matter where I was in the world or how I was living, I needed to have courage and trust that the situation I was in wouldn't last forever.

Every day is different, and the world is always changing. Tomorrow is a new day filled with new joy and prospects, all there is to do is to keep moving forward.

From an early age, I witnessed my family and the people around me fighting to keep their spirits high. They never surrendered, no matter how dark and dreary the world seemed. Even though I was very depressed and lonely, I was confident that I would prevail and enjoy the opportunity and freedom that I received. I just needed to remember to keep my spirits high, be brave, and never surrender. This was my strength. When life doesn't go the way you desired or expected, think of an alternative path and change directions. There must be a way to complete the task before you, and one way or another, it is up to you to be the master of your decisions and make the change you want to see in your life.

Fortunately, within a couple of months, I came across a small shop near the place I was staying. It was managed by a Canadian Baha'i who had lived in Halifax for over 20 years. I shared my story with them, relieved to be speaking so familiarly and connecting with others. After I had told them what I had gone through, I was invited to a regular Baha'i feast where local Baha'i gathered. I was shocked at how many people suddenly entered my life, surrounding me with warmth and willingness to assist or support me any way they could. It was the first time I felt relieved and safe. Among the many people I met, there were a couple in particular that I became very close with, Saied and Nadim.

Saied was a young Baha'i university student and to this day, we are still very good friends and keep in contact often. He had an enormous impact on my educational path and the learning process I went through in transitioning into life in Canada. Nadim, another university student, took me around Halifax and guided me through important matters in Halifax and the lifestyle here. Though I was only in Halifax for 7 months, he showed me the ropes of my new life. Nadim was kind enough to take me to Charlottetown, the capital of Prince Edward Island, where his parents lived. He would even drive me to other towns in Eastern Canada on the weekends sometimes. Both of these friends opened up my world and changed how I saw Halifax. My life was slowly starting to change, and the darkness that had haunted me when I first arrived was now turning into a brighter future.

Furthermore, I enrolled in an English language school which broadened the opportunities available to me. There were so many paths I could embark on, and my life expanded with possibilities. I not only met new people and friends at the school, but I was able to connect more with the community I was living in. However, despite all the good that was happening, there were still major challenges I had to overcome. Though my English was improving, I was still struggling to assimilate myself into the community.

I had no choice but to learn quickly and improve my understanding of other cultures and languages, and above all, their values in society and way of thinking. Canada was built on immigrants, and it was extraordinary to see so many people from diverse backgrounds living together in peace and harmony. Though I had yet to fully join the diverse community, I began to realize how blessed I was to live among them and to receive such a wonderful opportunity from this nation. I could learn so much from all of these people and through them, I could grow into my true potential. The opportunities and possibilities were endless, I just had to gain the right tools to utilize them.

My first goal and vision in Canada was to learn and become an integral part of the community. I wanted to be like them, so I applied myself more vigorously to my studies and my learning. I was eager to build a life for myself, filled with vision, and fight any difficulties that came my way. I learned how to look beyond the extremely cold winters and focus on enjoying the company around me. By putting aside my minor problem, I began to create a more colorful life where it didn't exist before. My future was becoming brighter, and I was becoming more confident, courageous and hopeful.

As I started getting my life organized and straightening out my priorities, I began to notice the hard work my friends at university and those working part-time jobs were doing. They were taking beneficial steps to build their life, but what was there for me to do? A year out of the refugee period and I had established a small community among the Canadian Baha'i, valuable friendships with extra activities, and started learning English, but what more could I do? Witnessing my friends working hard inspired me to work hard, too. They were the motivational directors in my life that encouraged me to do more and be more.

I wanted to uplift myself and flourish in a way that was different from others my age. Through established institutions, I would be given the tools to build a new life, comprehend the purpose of my life, and be guided to the next stage in my life. I decided to continue my education and focus on building my knowledge. However, starting a new chapter in life, especially that of education, wouldn't be easy. Though I had friends who encouraged me to follow this path and inspired me to be the best I could, I was alone in Canada and needed to take extra measures to protect myself. Continuing my education was a major decision, and though I was set on this vision, I needed to think long and hard about the change I was making in my life.

After 18 months of uncertainty and not being able to make a concrete decision about my future, I finally took the chance and moved to Montreal, Canada. Unlike the lack of opportunities that my previous town provided, there was more hope for my future in Montreal. I also was lucky that a few good friends and some distant relatives lived in this city.

After a couple of years of improving my English, I was finally able to apply for college. Quebec had a unique system where the first year of college is equivalent to grade 12 of high school. After finishing college, my second year was known as university. The system, while confusing, was a major setback on my path to higher education. I had already lost two important years of education during my time as a refugee, and another two years trying to settle down, learn English, and attend 12th grade, despite graduating 3 years younger than others my age in Iran. Though I was still young, time seemed to be slipping away from me. I had lost 4 years of my life to situations I couldn't change. Time, for me, was a crucial thing, and I look back on those 4 years wishing I could get them back so that I could use them as much as I could.

We are always chasing time and trying to get back the hours, days, or years we have lost. It is easy to get discouraged as time slips away and your vision seems like a vast canyon you have to cross but remember that you've made it this far. Despite all the struggles, obstacles, injustice, and hardship you had to face, you've survived today, so who is stopping you from striving tomorrow?

Life rarely works out the way we want it, our vision changes, we lose hope, but in the end, we have to remember to take the courageous first step. Once you've taken one step, the ones that follow become easier.

Though I had lost a significant amount of time, I threw myself into my goals and pushed myself to the limit. I wanted to do well in my education, and I wanted to learn and become one of the top students at my college. I couldn't let myself stray from my vision. To motivate myself, I would often think about my childhood, the person I wanted to become, and the direction I dreamed of taking. I kept in mind people like Gandhi, Pele, or animation heroes such as Marco Polo or Tin Tin, who made a difference in their life and the world they lived in. I held my love for football close, knowing that the effort I put into the sport had kept me intact and gave me the energy to work harder towards my goals. Though there wasn't much of a chance for me to excel in football considering Montreal was an ice hockey town, I was given the opportunity to play for my university's varsity team where I received a scholarship and worked hard towards my mental and physical health.

Sometimes it was hard to continue on my path towards vision when my loved ones weren't around to support me financially, morally, and physically. Their absence weighed on me, threatening my hope and my courage. The troublesome issues of making my own food, paying my own bills, dealing with rent and roommates had made their absence harder to bear. There were times when I would lose focus and not have the strength to continue on. I needed their support and their love, but our lives were on different paths. I did not have the luxury of the support of my family as some of my friends and peers did.

However, my life in itself was something of a miracle. Not everyone was lucky enough to survive four coups; not everyone was blessed with a family that loved them enough to let them go become a refugee; not everyone was given the opportunity to build a better life in a country that provided them safety and security. Reminding myself of all that I was grateful for in life and what I should value and not take for granted was what kept me hopeful, brave, and kept me going forward.

Even after my vision of becoming a professional football player failed, I fought on. I threw myself into my studies and looked at different paths' education could take me down. I wanted to expand my horizons and see the world through my education, and so I did. Throughout 14 years of higher education, I studied Law and International Affairs in the U.S., U.K., Australia, and Japan. I had the courage to reach for the stars despite my most treasured directors in my life being absent. The friends and mentors I've met helped build and shape my independent future.

I always considered myself blessed to be given the opportunity to restart my life from zero in Canada. Like Australia, New Zealand, Sweden and a few other countries, Canada was one of the best countries for refugees to immigrate to. Though I was an outsider and an immigrant, I was lucky to be in a country that had well-established and constructive methods towards long-term immigrants to integrate and settle into the nation with relative ease. Not only was Canada safe, comfortable, and peaceful, I felt welcomed into the country. Despite my rough start, I knew that Canada accepting my application was a high privilege. To embrace the life given to me, I needed to develop my vision even more and not lose hope. There was a plethora of opportunities in front of me and with the support of Farhoush, Ali, Farshid, Farid, Shahzad, Siavash, Shahin, Reza and many others, I was able to create a life for myself.

In the summer of 1998, 13 years after my independent journey, my dreams come true. I was reunited with my parents in Australia. They were different, I was different, but our love and respect for one another was something time couldn't take away from us. This moment was one of the most defining moments of my life. Seeing my parents motivated me to continue my education and begin the next stage in my journey. My newest vision was already taking shape from the moment I saw them, and I plan to become a global citizen where I could utilize my past, be a voice for those who have suffered as I have and support the younger generation as they go through unprecedented hardships in life. It would be a waste of space and life if I could not cherish and contribute to a world that is full of wonder to explore.

If I never had the dream and vision of living a bigger life, if I was never given hope from my parents that I could do *more* with my life and *be* more. If I never had the courage to take chances, I wouldn't have gotten to where I am now in my life. I was very fortunate for all that I was given in life, from my friends, my family, my mentors, and the country that gave me the chance to reach my true potential. We never know when we will be given life changing opportunities.

Sometimes, an opportunity doesn't seem so special when you're in the moment, but as time moves on, we realize how lucky we were to be given a chance to muster up our courage and go beyond. Sometimes I wonder how time flew by so quickly. The struggles in my life have changed from what they were in my youth and early adulthood, but every day is a fight for hope and a dare to have courage. Refugee and beyond was the key to the next chapter in my life. I took off to a place that gave me the means for a better future, landed with determination, hope, and courage, and then I will take off again to explore a different path to my life.

Reflection Activity

1. When was the last time that you felt courageous?

   _____

   _____

   _____

   _____

   _____

   _____

   _____

   _____

   _____

   _____

2. What were some struggles you've been through and how did you overcome them?

   _____

   _____

   _____

   _____

   _____

   _____

   _____

   _____

   _____

3. Was there ever a time in your life when you were at a fork in the road? How did you know which path to take and what was the outcome?

_____

_____

_____

_____

_____

_____

_____

_____

_____

4. Describe a defining moment in your life that made you who you are today.

_____

_____

_____

_____

_____

_____

_____

_____

_____

5. Who were the directors in your life that gave you courage or helped you when you struggled?

_____

_____

_____

_____

_____

_____

_____

_____

_____

6. How do you feel today and what can you do to make yourself feel more courageous?

_____

_____

_____

_____

_____

_____

_____

_____

Embark on your path with hope and courage as the wind that guides you forward! Believe in yourself even when dark thunderheads cloud your horizons because the future will break with blue skies and your resilience will be rewarded with a life painted in color.

Reflection Activity

PART FOUR

A Runway Towards the Future

Paying it Forward

Pursuing Vision

Since I was young, I have always searched for the meaning of life. I wondered what the reason was for existing, what happens after life, and I marveled at the colors that take shape in each of our lives and how we can use these colors to be remembered. My life has been one of struggle and grief. I've witnessed countless loved ones become banished, endure pain, and simply experience how brutal life could be. I survived through dark times, not knowing if there was anything waiting for me at the end of the tunnel. However, I've also found happiness and discovered how to thrive and live a life of wealth and joy. I am not a stranger to struggling and grief, but I also know what it is like to live comfortably and happily. I knew both sides of the coin and because of that, I was determined to do something about all the suffering and finally do something to help people. I wanted to take constructive action that not only stemmed from my thoughts and dissatisfaction in the world, but I want to pay tribute to those who have come before me and will exist after.

The trauma and life-changing events people face are numerous and the suffering in the world seems like an endless, dark well. However, if I could do something to brighten the days of those suffering or be the spark of hope they need to carry on, I would do as much as I could. I know the loneliness of losing family, a home, the directors in life, and struggle on the path of vision, hope and courage. I know how it is to feel like the darkest days will last forever, however, I also know that there is hope and happiness all around us. Even on my darkest days, there were people around me, struggling with their own problems, which took time out of their own life to lift me up and show me how to be hopeful and courageous.

Sometimes, those who face the deepest darkness are also the ones who are willing to share the little light they have nurtured within them. Despite all of the hardship, sorrow, and struggle, they taught me how to stand tall even when the world seems unbearable. A true star, shining with so much life and potential, bringing an aurora of color to other people's lives. That is what I want to give to others. That is what I want to pay forward.

Living in Canada, I learned practical and compelling ways to establish my vision. I realized that I could be a voice and support various initiatives that I was enthusiastic about. Back in Montreal, I had the opportunity to start a new adventure where I could take part in building valuable associations alongside other remarkable students in my years as an undergrad. I began to study more and learned new ways to be active in my vision. I began to create links with others throughout different societies at my university. I was a part of the Student Union, Southeast Asian Club, Persian Club, HIV Club, Chess Club, and a few others, hoping to connect with fellow students. I dedicated a lot of time and energy to these clubs, with the idea that I would meet others that shared my passion and would become a part of the change I wished to instill. The networks I created not only developed my knowledge, but allowed me to look beyond, into a deeper understanding of our world within.

While my extracurricular life was dedicated to these societies and groups, I was still engaged in pursuing higher education. I studied in different countries, and since I was alone, I was always looking for suitable institutions that provided me with the necessary scholarships and awards that would help pay for my schooling and living expenses. Everything I worked toward was for the prospect of a colorful future. I wanted to expand my knowledge and worldview so that I would be able to help others when the time came. I grew my network and understanding of others so that I would be able to make a difference in the people I meet.

It took days, months, even years to build something worth fighting for. The right time and place were crucial when implementing my thoughts and experience into something tangible. Though I built a network during my years as an undergrad, it wasn't until I took off and started my career as a graduate in Japan where I finally found the right time and place to implement my vision. While Japan is a highly developed country in terms of technology along with being one of the wealthiest and safest places, I began to witness some issues within the infrastructure of society, especially education of the younger generations.

I came to Japan for graduate school in 1999, and though I had backpacked through the country for three months a few years prior, it was when I was living in Japan that I noticed the prospect of a beginning for my vision. Before coming to Japan, I had studied and traveled to over 30 countries. In my time living in each place, I've realized that no country or place is perfect, and every society has its faults. However, the issues I found in Japan inspired me to want to make a change.

I found that there were problems among the youth that were quite disturbing. It was shocking to learn that the statistics for Japanese children suffering from mental health issues were high compared to other developed and emerging countries. The high suicide rate in Japan due to low satisfaction in their young life was astonishing. I couldn't help but reflect on my own life and all the struggle and hardship I had experienced and encountered. Alongside my ponderings about mental health, I began to grow more curious about Japan, wondering why this country has had trouble broadening their ways and why there was reluctance in welcoming refugees.

It was simply the act of being curious about Japanese society that ignited my vision. I could feel that this country was a place where I would be able to grow my ideas and the dream I was slowly formulated. I was still a student attending graduate school and between my part time job, a social life, and studying, I wasn't ready to establish a vision that would take off and make a difference. It was just a thought that I hadn't honed nor shaped it into something coherent. It was a vision that would unfold over time.

Though I was inspired by Japanese society, another passion of mine that I had nurtured and involved myself with throughout my undergraduate education in Canada was my passion for fashion and colors. There were several occasions where I worked with the fashion industry as a model or as staff on a runway show. I was enthralled by the color and exuberance of life in fashion. Even when coming to Japan for graduate school, I still sought out work in the colorful world of the fashion industry. Throughout my years of being involved with fashion and runway shows, I learned how flashy and eye-catching the industry is. I highly respected those I worked for and keenly observed how attractive and exclusive the fashion world is compared to other industries.

Sometimes it is in the most unlikely combination that we find beauty and hope. Never give up on yourself or your dream just because it is unusual or out of the ordinary. Dare to make a change by being the change.

Since I was a child, I always had a sharp eye for fashion. I notice how my father and mother always dress so fashionably, presenting themselves in a well-kept manner. They were constantly donning colorful clothes and often wore crisp, fancy dresses or suits and black ties when attending diplomatic or official functions. I was always mesmerized by the sense of style they had and the way they would carry themselves in their clothing. During those times, when my family lived peacefully, I grew to be very impressed and proud of their lifestyle. The power of fashion was remarkable, and though I didn't consciously chase my passion for fashion, it found me later in life, reminding me of a time when my family was whole and living in peace.

As I reached the end of my higher education, I realized that I didn't want to sacrifice my passion for fashion and color to build my vision to make a change and help others -- and vice versa. These two aspirations, though vastly different, were no less important than the other. I needed to find a way to bridge them together and build a system that could unite and narrow the gap between these two worlds. Even as a child, I had always noticed the steep gap between the rich and the poor. Why were the poor so poor? What could *I* do to mend the gaping hole between these two worlds?

Fashion and runway shows are usually thought of as high society, while building a project or foundation that helps the poor is often deemed as a lower, more humble profession. But why does it have to be one over the other? Above anything else, my vision was to raise awareness on the issues that I have experienced (losing my home, being separated from loved ones, being thrown into chaos during times of war, and facing misery) and connect with millions of other people and children that are going through the same thing. I wanted to bridge the gap by bringing the awareness of misfortune, poverty, displacement, refuge, and expulsion to the world of fashion and beauty.

However, to fulfill my vision and make it succeed, I needed to know more about Japan. Though I studied in the country, there were still many things I didn't know. It took years to establish a plan, but since I was determined to make a change and follow through with my vision, I didn't hold back. I did my research, planned and prepared aspects I wanted to go into my vision, and carefully combed through regulations and resources I needed to build something that would last forever. If I were to build something with my own two hands, I wanted it to be something I could leave behind.

As I began piling the stepping stones to create a foundation, I started to notice many cultural differences and obstacles that I hadn't faced before. After dedicating so much time and energy into this vision, it finally accumulated into something tangible. However, launching my vision was something I couldn't do on my own, so I built a team. I recruited individuals who understood the concept of my vision and complemented the mission well. Building and maintaining the right team is one of the most important factors to a successful organization, so I took due diligence to make the right team, a dedicated one.

On Course

In early 2010, with the help of passionate people, dedicated friends, and university students, Runway for Hope (RFH) was founded. Though it took nearly a decade to create this foundation, I kept faith that everything would work out in the end, and I put my vision into action. The time and effort that I had poured into this project finally paid off and I was excited to see my goal turn into a tangible and legitimate organization. I knew that the creation of this foundation would be a lifetime commitment filled with long-term responsibilities, but it was worth it. My keen interest for fashion and dedication to helping others was finally bridged into one, encompassing organization.

The name and motto *Make Life Colorful* was something that had been in the back of my head for years before the establishment of this entity. Runway for Hope's slogan, *Make Life Colorful*, not only presents what we believe and stand for, but it also relates to what we connect and associate with. We strive to be exceptional and one of a kind. We want to take action and make a change that would support the underprivileged and those facing hardship. Instead of organizing a marathon, cooking event, a fundraiser with a band, or hosting a small party, we wanted to do something that is truly original and catch attention. We wanted our organization to be unique, so we decided to bring awareness by hosting a runway show as one of the main mediums.

Our mission and vision sounded monumental and phenomenal. We had big goals and ideas that we hoped would educate our surrounding society successfully. We knew it would take time, especially in Japan, but we were willing to do whatever it took to make sure Runway for Hope was blooming. We had an important message to share, and we were determined for this message to be heard in an array of colors. Those involved in the world of fashion would recognize the incredible energy it took to build a runway show lasting just less than 20 minutes, but would the rest of Japan understand the hard work it took to share our message?

My goal was to utilize my decade of experience in the fashion industry to really launch the foundation. Before establishing the organization, I had put together several workshops and study sessions in order to understand and learn more about effective strategies when generating a concept for the runway. On my path towards my vision, I took the initiative to reach out to globally recognized brands such as Gucci, CD, Hugo Boss, Channel, Issey Miyake, Valentino, Koshino Hiroko, Roberto Cavalli and a few others. It was an intimidating step in my plan to build my own organization and it took a lot of time and effort, but I was determined to make the foundation the best that it could be. Though I was rejected by all of the brands I had reached out to, I did not give up.

Workshops, Seminars 2009, 2010

The questions that I had asked since I was a child, the dreams I had failed, and the directors in my life that both supported me and pushed me to do better, I wanted to prove and show that I could do it. I began approaching renowned stylists, stage managers, directors, and recognized producers who were the key to building a high quality and unforgettable runway show. Reaching out to big brands and well-known people in the fashion industry was taking a big leap of faith and it tested my patience and my determination towards my vision. I was faced with many rejections and sometimes even ignored. Most were not interested in this unique approach to bringing awareness through a fashion show. The expectations I had versus the reality I was faced with diverged.

I began to realize the lack of awareness and global understanding that many people had. It was evident why the gap between the rich and the poor was so excessive, everyone was in their own little bubble, and no one wanted to leave. Even so, I was persistent and wouldn't let that deter my vision. However, with each rejection letter I faced, the ideas I had to promote my foundation were dwindling. I had to come up with different plans and strategies that were persuasive and attractive to those who otherwise wouldn't give my proposition a second glance. I wouldn't give up so easily.

Determination is the key when approaching your vision and being competitive at a professional level in order to overcome the unexpected obstacles that try to prevent your success.

Deep inside, I knew and believed that the platform and business model of RFH was something truly unique. I had faith that the runway show would be a fantastic avenue that would bring awareness to the cause I was advocating for. Backing down wasn't an option and I had to find other ways to make the foundation flourish if one plan failed. There were other ideas I was eager to implement within Runway for Hope, but I needed to be patient and focus on getting the foundation off the runway before touching down on different landing strips. As I've learned throughout my lifetime, a small amount of patience can go a long way. It is the key to any successful project and endeavor. I needed to be focused, encourage my team and remind everyone that the plan we were following was important. To make others' lives more colorful, we first need to succeed *within* before we can make a difference *without*.

There were many obstacles that got in the way of the foundation's success. Though we had established ourselves as a nonprofit organization, we had to be aware of the boundaries and restraints that prohibited our foundation. Especially as a foreigner in Japan creating a constructive entity designed with global vision, I had to take care in what I did and work harder to hold my vision together. It was a massive task that seemed impossible, but despite the boundaries, bureaucracies, and traditional processes that held me back and slowed my progress towards my goal, I still had hope for a brighter future.

Just because something seems impossible, daunting, and hard doesn't mean that it isn't worth it. Life is filled with challenges that we have to overcome. It isn't how *fast* we overcome them, but *how* we overcome them is the key. Nonetheless, despite all the challenges I faced, I was fortunate to launch one of my biggest dreams and passions in Japan. Though the process of building a venture or an organization in Japan might take longer than any other countries, there is a fierce loyalty, dedication and reliability that I've found here worth fighting for.

Despite all the obstacles the organization faced, there were directors in my life that supported me, and many people who extended their hope for our success and imparted positivity and words of wisdom. These people, along with the Runway for Hope team, made all the struggles worth it. I owe my success to my dedicated team as well as those who believed in me. Their support and sincerity in the foundation gave me the hope and courage to face all the questions and doubts I received from many individuals and corporations I had approached.

Why put together a runway show in support of internally displaced and underprivileged children?

Some people and various companies couldn't understand why our foundation was trying to tie an upper-class event with a social justice cause. These people couldn't see the relation between the two worlds. How we were going to build our vision and where we planned to take it was called into question many times. People wondered what runway shows and fashion had to do with helping those less fortunate or what the purpose of our foundation was. Our response was that Runway for Hope is a 'PATH.' Our foundation is a path in life, an *enlightenment*. Whether under spotlights stuttering or at an airport waiting, the runway is an opportunity to seize an incredible journey. Take off and look towards the horizon! The future awaits, filled with color and prospects. Runway for Hope is a journey that takes you beyond introducing you to the question: *how to live life?*

At the end of the day, why not? Why not build a high-end fashion show to support and bring awareness to the hardships around the world? Why not attempt to merge a growing gap in society? Why not take a chance? Because at the end of the day, when all is said and done, you don't want to regret not taking the first step in a colorful life. Revel in the pleasure of an accomplishment and be happy that you tried.

There will always be people who will question and doubt your abilities but remember this: You shouldn't need a reason to want to help and support those who are suffering. You don't need a reason to do what you love. If there is an opportunity in front of you, available and easy to grasp, take it.

Nonetheless, we used the obstacles and skepticism we received to propel our organization forward. Gathering people's opinions and feedback, we were able to improve and create a better version of our foundation. Those who supported and helped our organization grow were truly the heart of what makes RFH what it is today.

I knew that fashion would be a wonderful vehicle and creative outlet to merge the world of luxury with the world of hardship. It was a challenge to build a constructive team and even more so to pick Runway for Hope off the ground and launch it into the air, but despite our challenges, I knew that giving up and turning back wasn't an option. We would make the world colorful and support those facing darkness and hardship. Producing runway shows that would illuminate the hardships and put a spotlight on those suffering was not a simple feat to achieve, however, it made the most spirited and colorful impact that anyone could have imagined.

A runway show is a piece of art that tells a story. In the setting of a cold and unfamiliar stage, colors, patterns, and emotions come to life as models walk up the runway in extraordinary clothes.

Each piece is a part of a larger story that designers weave for their audience. It is an incapacitating and spectacular experience. It isn't just the models that walk on stage that do all of the work, nor is it the designers who dream up designs or tailors and seamstresses that put them all together. There are so many people backstage who are involved in the success of a 15 to 20 minutes show.

The Timekeeper, who weaves in each model on the stage, fighting against the dwindling time of the show. The Stage Manager, directing and taking care of everything that is the stage, including the models and team. The Choreographer, who livens up the show by creating routines and movement sequences for a more captivated audience. The Director and Producer, without whom, the show wouldn't be able to go on. Then there are the Assistant Stage Manager, MC, Make-Up Artists, Hair Stylists, Fitters, Photo and Videographer, Operational Staff and other staff working methodically to put together an unforgettable and a perfect show. In a decent fashion show with 10 - 20 models, there can be over 50 people backstage that you never see. Without all of these people working tirelessly to put the show together, the extravaganza of a runway show wouldn't exist. We shouldn't take for granted the hard work and effort that we cannot see.

It is all a part of the journey, the path of life. Sometimes you need to workdays, months, even years to create something that only lasts 15 minutes. The hard work might seem endless, and discouragement might be a close friend, but at the end of it all is something amazing -- something only you could create. It isn't just the hard work you pour into a project that makes it successful, it is believing in yourself, staying determined, having faith, being courageous, and most importantly: having directors in your life that support and encourage you.

The story of our runway isn't just the amazing and hardworking team that puts the magic of a runway together, it is the displaced children who have nowhere else to go, the suffering kids have to witness at such a young age, and the hardship that they will have to struggle and strive through all their life. Together, we bridge the gap and make something beautiful, colorful, and long-lasting.

'It isn't how FAST you reached here, it's HOW you reached here fast.'

When we first began our foundation, there were only a marginal number of refugees living in Japan. Refugees from Myanmar, Afghanistan, Iraq, and later Syria were some of the select few that were given permission to enter Japan. Unlike some European countries, Australia, Canada and the U.S., Japan's reluctance in accepting refugees has been a highly political issue revolving around the government's hesitancy to open its borders. Despite there not being many refugees in Japan, I wanted to use my knowledge and experience to change the refugee situation in Japan. I was a refugee in the past and I even had a degree in writing on immigration, security and displacement-related matters. I felt that it was within my power to do something meaningful

I met with senior team members of other non-profit organizations that were reliable and committed to helping the causes. I heard their voices, did my own research, and came to a conclusion on how the Japanese public and Japanese government would react towards refugees and foreigners. The results I found were completely different to what I had experienced in the many different countries I had lived in before settling in Japan.

The world of Japan was a completely different culture and way of thinking than I was used to. Despite major cities in Japan evolving and modernizing, societal thought had yet to change much from 500 years ago. The island of Japan has preserved its traditional culture to the utmost. Other than reputable foreigners who enter legally to work, study, or reside in Japan, I found that many Japanese didn't want to jeopardize their livelihood and peaceful community by opening the borders to others.

While the answers shocked me, I could understand their reasoning. Japan is one of the safest and most comfortable places to live, and while I admire the idea of a safe community, I couldn't help but remember the two years I waited at the refugee camp, waiting for my turn to go off and start a better life. How many refugees are there now, fleeing from prosecution, hardship, and turmoil? How many people are being forced to leave their homes with nowhere else to go but seek shelter at refugee locations? I think about my experience, the friends I made at the camps, the refugees I interviewed during my post-graduate work. I think of Salman and all that he lost. How we would all give anything for a slice of security and comfort.

Japan has one of the highest financial contributions to the United Nations, UNHCR, UNICEF, and they are among the top contributors to the Global Fund to fight diseases as well as a major ODA (Official Development Assistance) funding to support international development and infrastructure. Japan exports many funds to aid those in need, however, it is ironic that this country never imports those that need the most help. There is a hesitancy to let refugees enter Japan, and though it has been proven that refugees could contribute to improving nations, there is no policy allowing refugees into the country. To name a few, Albert Einstein, Mahatma Gandhi, Sigmund Freud, Steve Jobs, and Freddie Mercury were all refugees who had distinguished themselves from society in a positive way. They have helped social development, economy, infrastructure, science and technology all because they were given the chance to start anew in a different country when their livelihood was taken away from them.

Aside from famous refugees throughout history, there are many highly successful and distinguished former refugees that have made a name for themselves in many industries all over the world. The idea that refugees bring insecurities and problems to the nations they immigrate to is a biased notion. These people gave up their lives, their home, and risked their safety to make it to a country where they could hope to have a better life. Accepting refugees and displaced peoples into our country makes us better and our society more colorful.

Former Refugees (left to right: Albert Einstein, Alek Wek, Freddie Mercury)

After observing these unprecedented issues, I shared my thoughts with my team. Our foundation was fighting an uphill battle, and we needed to branch out if we were going to be successful. Before we grew too ambitious in supporting various initiatives and solving another country's problems, we needed to clean our own house first. We decided to turn our focus towards helping locals who suffered hardship instead. We put in the work where it was needed and with many activities, unique projects, and Runway for Hope's annual show, we were quite busy.

Since our foundation also circulated around fashion, beauty and art, we supported younger talent artists, models, and hair/make-up artists who didn't receive opportunities to perform and shine previously. This was an important aspect of the runway platform and channels related to. Not only did we want to help refugees and those facing hardship and suffering, but it was important for RFH to nurture the younger generation and give them the opportunity to grow. We provided them with our career platform, linking them with overseas experts and affiliates as well as offering awards and scholarships. These weren't just inexperienced individuals we were taking chances on; they were aspiring professionals who soaked up all our foundation had to offer, and in return, they provided us with fresh, original viewpoints. RFH was quickly growing and expanding, reaching and inspiring others to lead a more colorful life.

However, on March 11th, 2011, a little over one year after RFH was founded, Japan suffered from a 9.1 magnitude earthquake that was followed by the strongest tsunami ever recorded in the Tohoku region. This natural disaster left the Japanese population in shambles. More than 20,000 people lost their lives and over 470,000 people were internally displaced, forced to find temporary housing. The tsunami reached heights of up to 40.5 meters (133 ft.) in Miyako Iwate Prefecture and traveled at over 700 km/h (435 mph) and up to 10 km/h (6 mph) inland. The devastation and destruction were unforgettable.

Most of the suffering and struggle in my life had come from human-induced events. Due to war, revolutions, and coups, I lived a life that was constantly changing from one struggle to another. However, being in Japan during the time of the earthquake, I experienced first-hand how terrifying and horrific a natural disaster could be. Refugees and displaced people never leave their homes because they want to, but because they are *forced* to. Either from natural disasters or human violence, there are people who are constantly looking for a better life.

For all the times I had witnessed others suffering, unable to do anything, this was one of the biggest moments in my life where I was able to do something to ease the hardship occurring. Coming to Japan for graduate school in 1999, I was beyond grateful and fortunate to be nominated and awarded a very generous scholarship along with other benefits. Though when I came back to Japan in 2004 to create my foundation, I was faced with many obstacles. This country had given me so much and I had so many fond memories that when the natural disaster hit, there was nothing more important to me than to be there for all the displaced people. With all the friends and amazing people, I worked with, I felt indebted to this country that I had worked so hard in. I had gained so much living in Japan that it was now time for me to give back what I could.

However, since it was a major catastrophe and the government was redirecting resources to the affected areas, unauthorized personnel were not allowed to enter towns where the tsunami had hit. Watching the news was unbearable; people were in grief and hardship and the strong desire I felt to help was making me anxious. Despite these towns being blocked off from civilians, I did not lose hope nor was I discouraged at the obstacles before me.

I was more determined than I ever was to act instead of waiting around.

With the help and bravery of a friend, we made the drive to the north and two towns that had been hit by the tsunami. The damage was heart-wrenching and thousands of lives were lost. We stayed for over a week, helping locals with meals, cleaning rubbish, working with other volunteers to clean the cemeteries, and much more physical labor wherever we could help.

Though we busied ourselves with helping around the town, it was painful to see all the destruction and ruin. Houses and tombstones were demolished, memories of those who had lived in the city were nothing but rubble. It reminded me of my past and the struggle I saw during the Iran and Iraq war. The houses of my aunts and uncles that were burnt down and destroyed after the Iran Revolution. There were so many people running from prosecution, losing their lives trying to flee, either by unsuccessfully passing through the border or downing trying to make it across the sea and river. So much of my past and what had happened on March 11th were the same yet vastly different, lives were lost, houses and livelihoods in shambles, panicked people trying to make sense of the destruction around them.

Volunteering - post Tsunami, Iwanuma, Tohoku Region - 5/2011

"We make a living by what we get, but we make a life by what we give"

-Winston Churchill

Like several other moments in my past, this was a heartbreaking experience I had witnessed. Because of the path in life that I had walked and the experiences I had gone through, I felt kindred to these people. I sympathize with them and wanted to be there for them in any way that I could. I saw myself in many children I came across, without a home and suffering from the loss of loved ones. The pain I felt for them was unbearable. I wanted to help, but there was only so much I could do. The trauma and suffering they had endured would be something that they would have to carry around for the rest of their lives.

To this day, the earthquake and tsunami of March 11th, 2011 is still one of the most painful periods in my life. There have been so many people and friends that have still not been able to return to their home and are displaced, living in tiny and uncomfortable conditions. Though I had done what I could and helped where I was able, there was still so much pain and suffering that was left unattended.

However, one positive thing that came out of the horrifying tragedy was that this horrible occurrence gave Runway for Hope a new mission to set out on. Everyone was passionate to help and the mind frame and motivation we all felt to do something for those suffering overtook the heart of our foundation. RFH not only began to raise funds for the disaster, but we also worked with the local government, offering our educational programs, supporting locals with repatriation programs, helping with career building for the youth along with Study Abroad and Tokyo Summer Programs as a part of Runway for Hope's *Life Design* scheme.

Despite our new initiative of helping and supporting those who had lost their homes and loved ones, and were now displaced, we realized it might be impossible to have globally renowned brands featured on the runway aspect of our foundation. While we were fortunate enough to be helping out those in need, we had yet to bridge the gap between fashion and those suffering. Instead of waiting around for the chance that a well-known brand would partner with us, we decided to build our own runway show. However, this wouldn't be a small feat.

Not only did I have experience as a model and staff of a runway show, I also had experience directing and producing several runway shows, both for personal and professional endeavors. However, even with experience, I knew that creating a runway show of our own was going to be an incredibly challenging project. If we were going to have to deal with pure branding and fashion ideas, we needed to utilize our own expertise and network. Instead of high-end brands, we decided to support young, talented designers looking for a beak in the industry. Bridging the societal gap between fashion and hardship and being true to our mission of supporting the next generation, our runway show and foundation would truly be a unique experience that we hoped everyone would want to be a part of.

Our team worked hard to make the fashion show a success. We had people with expertise in fashion, stage management, production, choreographers, and so many more. We were not just creating a show for fundraising purposes, but also to support upcoming designers and artists. As we planned and prepared for our runway show, we were already getting acknowledged by the public. People outside the foundation were getting excited for the fashion show just as much as we were eagerly anticipating the launch day.

We recruited and increased our team, hiring young, recently graduated makeup artists and hair stylists as well as photographers and videographers. After many years of going through highs and lows in life, traveling and living in various countries, meeting so many people and learning about different cultures around the world, I realized that life is similar to a runway show. We work hard to build a vision that could take years, and an ample amount of time and energy to come to fruition. The staff hired to build the runway show are like the directors in our lives, each person playing a special role in the outcome of our vision and without them, we wouldn't be able to reach our final goal. Despite the adversaries we go through in building our vision, there comes a time when all of our time and effort has paid off.

The gratification of completing your runway is one of the most important times in your life; it is the accumulation of all those in your life that have supported you along the way, your vision that you've worked tirelessly to fulfill, and the opportunity to take off again. With the right team, directors, supporters around you, you are not alone on your path to success. When you fall down, they are the ones to give you hope and motivate you to have courage. There is perfection in imperfect pieces coming together to help and support one another. I couldn't have built Runway for Hope alone. I am not perfect, I cannot do everything all on my own, but together, with a hardworking and passionate team, along with all of the commuted donors, supporters, and affiliates, Runway for Hope was on the right track.

Our vision and plan to support those in need became more important than ever. Alongside the annual runway show, we visited those who were suffering from hardship and spent quality time with displaced children. Though the situation seemed bleak, these encounters and moments were filled with color. The joy and playfulness among the children could almost make you forget their situation. We were not just helping them, but they were also helping me and members of our team.

Kamaishi and Ofunato city, Iwate prefecture, Japan

There is nothing more valuable and colorful than giving unbound affection and receiving hugs and smiles from a child with a pure heart.

Talk about our initiative and platform made it all the way to Taiwan, Singapore, Korea, China, US, Australia, Myanmar, and several other countries. The important work that we were doing and the color we were bringing to the world was finally getting noticed.

My small dream of bridging the gap between the world of fashion and a world of hardship had grown, just as I was confident that it would. I was offered involvement in two globally recognized beauty pageants as a National Director in Japan, Korea and Myanmar. This was a once in a lifetime opportunity not only for me to support these other organizations with my experience, but it was a chance for me to expand my network on behalf of RFH. With the help of a handful of devoted friends, I was able to work for both RFH and as a National Director for the pageants.

During this stage in my life, I was lucky to explore other interests during my extensive travels. I was able to meet many distinguished personalities on top of expanding my knowledge for my professional career. I have been very blessed to exist in this life, surrounded by wonderful people and many friends. Living in a world of color has so many different meanings; before the start of our foundation, my world was colored differently. The colors in my life have grown more vibrant since those days in the Iranian and Pakistan's desert, wondering if I would ever see my family again or if I would survive the perilous journey.

I am forever grateful for those who had supported me and gave me hope. I have come a long way in my life and it is almost unbelievable how much has changed. Life is never what we expect. We could wake up to a perfectly normal world, but the next day, it could all come crashing down. Tomorrow is never a promise, so do what you can today and who knows, maybe all of our struggling and striving could pay off in the future.

As for me, the experience doing the beauty pageant had provided me with more insight and other opportunities that I could share with Runway for Hope. I was always looking for new ways to better the foundation and constantly planning on launching new programs that could benefit children and their futures. Education is by far one of the most important factors in making a change in this world. My team and I were highly committed to building a program and a world dedicated to learning through first-hand experience. I was fortunate to have so many teachers that were wonderful directors in my life that I wanted to do the same. I wanted to pay forward the lessons and impact that they had on me and my vision at a young age.

Pursuing Vision

Life Design
Path to Enlightenment

Since the beginning of Runway for Hope, I always had so many ideas about how the foundation could be used to help children and guide them how to live their life to the fullest. Between the runway show bringing attention to refugees and our ground efforts in helping others post-disaster, I was extremely happy with what Runway for Hope had become during its first couple years. However, growing up and watching how my father and mother always helped people, how my teachers had helped me with my vision, and finally building a team at Runway for Hope that was dedicated to helping others, I knew that we could do more. I wanted to pay forward all of the kindness, wisdom, opportunity, and chances I received from the directors in my life. I wanted to create a life design that not only helped children achieve greatness, but helped parents become closer to their kids.

When we had finally begun to initiate our study abroad program in 2015, I knew that we were on the right track to doing more and helping more children. This program was just the start of our vision within the foundation. However, during the start of our study abroad program, *Life Design* wasn't more than an idea that spearheaded our study abroad program.

After years of experience and accumulating achievements through Runway for Hope, everything our team worked hard on over the years had finally boiled down to the creation of this important initiative. In 2019 we were able to create this important educational advancement program for children and early youth that we called: Life Design. Though our Life Design program was created after the study abroad and summer programs, the ideas and missions to each were all encompassing.

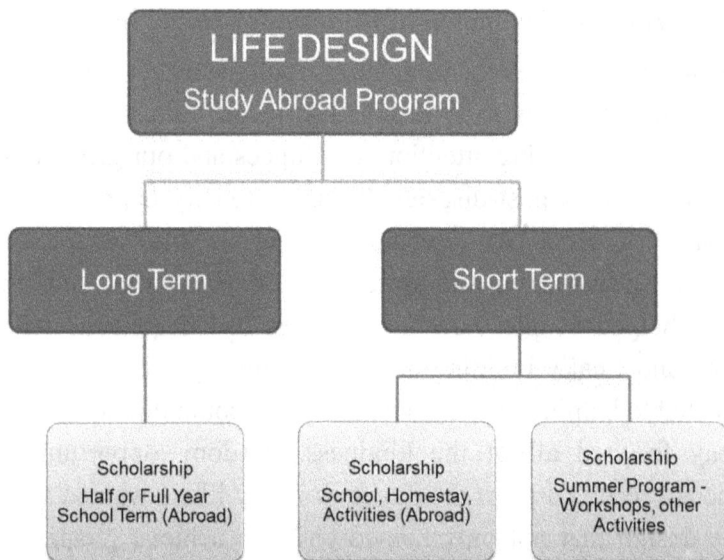

```
                    ┌─────────────────────────┐
                    │      LIFE DESIGN        │
                    │  Study Abroad Program   │
                    └─────────────────────────┘
                ┌──────────────┴──────────────┐
        ┌───────────────┐            ┌───────────────┐
        │   Long Term   │            │   Short Term  │
        └───────────────┘            └───────────────┘
```

Scholarship Half or Full Year School Term (Abroad)	Scholarship School, Homestay, Activities (Abroad)	Scholarship Summer Program - Workshops, other Activities

Life Design was created to be a tailored program that consists of unique cross-disciplinary courses, programs, runway, and workshops that were designed to be one of a kind in Japan. Our vision for this program was to build goodwill, safety, and happiness among all the children and youth in the world. We designed this program to improve the overall development of students and ensure they were receiving a well-rounded education. It reflects the goals and visions of Runway for Hope, while also highlighting our unique areas of specialization and innovation.

The Life Design program is so much more than a curriculum that students will merely learn and forget as they get older. Life Design is an *experience* that provides students the tools they need to take off into the world and find their own vision and purpose in life. This program is highly unique, having considerable flexibility built in to fit different classrooms and students, while still ensuring coverage of all the important curriculums. Life Design encourages positive individual development, student responsibility, co-operation, creativity, and respect for individuals and equality amongst them. Uniquely, this program is geared to benefit both the needs of the children along with parents.

Study Abroad Program - A World filled with Colors

Benefits of Studying Abroad:

- More responsibility, co-operation, creativity, and respect for individuality along with racial and gender equality
- Learn about other cultures and lifestyles
- Overcoming hardship and having hope
- Building skills in leadership, life innovation, self-reliance, and resilience
- Preparing for a brighter life and/or career
- Encouraging positive individual development
- Enrich young, global minds
- Building a bridge for the future
- Just having fun *living*

In 2015, Runway for Hope decided to finally initiate the long-awaited Study Abroad Program that we had been working on and building for the last couple years. The program would provide full scholarships to selected Junior and High school students in hardship. Though we had been working hard on our annual runway show, fundraising activities, meeting with victims and those facing hardships, educational workshops, and various guest speaker presentations, we decided to pay it forward even more with this new program.

Since we had already built an overseas network and prepared the necessary tools to complete the amazing program, we thought it was time to implement it. Our goal and hope for this program was for these students to truly benefit from being global through various walks in their life. This program would create an enormous impact on a student's education, career, and overall life path. As we raised funds through different channels and established donors, we allocated scholarships to the students who had been selected for the program. The scholarships paid for their airfare, homestay, food, health insurance, language school and all tailored activities.

The response our program got from students all over Japan was overwhelming. Despite Japan being renowned for its wealth, safety and technological advancements, there are still so many students who have faced adversaries and hardships. After receiving the applications, we did a screening on the students before the initial interview where they introduced themselves and their life. The students who passed the introduction interview then moved onto the main interview where they told us what they hoped to get out of the program and what their vision was.

Once candidates were selected, we began preparing them for the program. We provided online workshops where they could learn more about where they were going, preparing for what to expect from a foreign country, along with some useful language skills that could help them get around in an English-speaking country. Most of these students had never even left their town before. They were all from the countryside and to have the opportunity to go abroad and experience something beyond what they knew was a dream come true for most of the students.

For the first two years of the program, we took a number of students to Albany, Oregon in the U.S. for a 10 days study trip. We worked directly with the local language school who prepared all the activities and extracurriculars that we had agreed upon. Along with a tailored program, the homestay families the students stayed with were considerate, kind, and gave the students a once in a lifetime experience.

Study Abroad Program - Oregon, U.S 2016, 2017

However, we wanted to do even more for these kids. We wanted to show our sincerity towards their global studies and provide them with tools to build stronger relationships. These students weren't just statistics going through the program at RFH, their future was much more important to us and we wanted to make sure that the students knew that. As someone who had lost a lot in life at a young age and left behind loved ones and the security of a home, I wanted to provide these students with the full support of RFH and give them the opportunity to grow and thrive.

The third year of the program, we received an offer to visit Sydney, Australia where we worked on improving the program. We added core values to the program, focusing more on life design - an educational and career purpose. The program wasn't just to go to language school and have fun exploring and immerse themselves in a different culture, but we wanted the students to nurture an educational and career-shaping experience that would empower their future and create leaders that will one day make the world a better place. We wanted them to be able to learn self-reliance and resilience so they could turn that into motivation.

Aside from collaborating with the language school in Sydney, we wanted to make the two weeks trip worthwhile. Since we had established core values for the program, we wanted to take action and start implementing our new and improved vision. We approached our contacts and sponsors in Australia, some of whom were multinational corporations that had business based in Australia. Luckily for us, each one of our contacts had graciously offered their services and wanted to assist our program.

Study Abroad – Sydney, Australia
Macquarie Group Ltd., Global Headquarter

After contacting some of the corporations and requesting them to prepare a few hours for touring and short presentations about the company's values and professional lifestyle, we were able to get our students first-hand experience into the professional world. During the two-week program, the students were also privileged to meet with the Consul-General of Japan in Australia who talked about how he started his career at foreign affairs. He shared with them the value of representing his countries, the responsibilities involved, and the beauty of being a public servant.

Our two weeks in Australia was more than we could have hoped for. My colleague and I could see the light and amazement in the students' eyes as they learned more about different avenues their future could have. The questions they had for the Consul General and the wonderful experience they had in meeting with some of the executives of the major corporations in Sydney were moments in their lives that would stick with them forever. We could just see the positivity that radiated from the group, and we hoped that this would be just a stepping stone for future students in the study abroad program.

Among all of our curriculums and programs that we designed for study abroad, our homestay program was one of the most distinctive. This program was not just a typical overseas trip for the children to learn English. As part of the 'Life Design' scheme, the study abroad program was designed to give students, who had experienced hardship, the opportunity to gain valuable lessons that they can take with them throughout life in spite of the hardship they faced. We wanted the students to not only be able to go to a different country and experience a different culture and language, but we also wanted the students to have the most immersive experience that they could. To broaden their vision, build a network, create good directors for their life and their careers, and on top of it all, be resilient, 'Life Design' was created.

Runway for Hope's Study Abroad Program was not designed to be like some other organization that had an ample amount of funds and sent 100 or 1,000 students abroad each year. What RFH offered was a more intimate and unique experience where the students were placed with a family who had come to Australia as an immigrant with a refugee background. Since voices of refugees in Japan weren't well heard, this was a great opportunity for young, bright students to learn about the struggles these families had to go through in order to find solace. The students, too, had experienced some sort of hardship in their lives, so for them to meet families that had strived for a better life with hope and courage, hopefully sparked inspiration within them.

Like many refugees, these homestay families left behind a home, life, and memories in order to immigrate to Australia where they had to start their life from zero once again. One of the families had come to Australia in their 60s, having to rent an apartment, go to language school, find their way around the community, register for health insurance, retake their driver's license and so many other things. They were already well into their life when they had to start all over again in a new country and new environment.

Host families, Sydney - Australia 2018

These families were a source of hope and inspiration for the Japanese students that stayed with them. The children could see that they were not the only ones going through difficulties and a loss of hope. To build a new life takes strength and courage, especially since many of these families had spent many decades building their own life before having to start back at square one. These families were filled with motivation to make the most of the new life they were given, and we hoped that the students would respect and appreciate the hard work these families put into making a life for themselves. From a personal viewpoint, meeting these families had also moved me. I was reminded of Salman and all the people in my life that have struggled and strove for a better future.

However, for the students, staying with a homestay family for the first time can be daunting. At the beginning of the program, we let the students get comfortable and acquainted with their host families, though they are a bit shy and distant the first couple of days. After the third day of the program, we often hear that they open up to their host families, trying to communicate the best they can despite English being a big obstacle. Despite the struggle in communication, the children learn to convey what they feel and by the end of the program, they have made deep connections with their homestay family.

"People will forget what you said, people will forget what you did, but people will never forget how you made them feel."

-Maya Angelou

From runway shows to study abroad programs to being sponsored by some amazing organizations and countries, our foundation was quickly drawing attention from many countries. Though our start was a rocky one, we eventually started getting dedicated supporters and affiliates from all over the world. We received offers from other countries to host our students in Italy, Finland and Canada. The opportunities we got to pay it forward were beginning to seem innumerable.

Career Development
Summary Program
Summer Program

Along with our flourishing Study Abroad program, in 2019 we began creating a domestic summer program in Tokyo. We were lucky to receive support from our existing sponsors and individual donors, making the process to design and initiate the program much easier. As part of the 'Life Design' scheme, this program was also designed to give students the opportunity to seize their future and do the most that they can with their life. Similar to the process for our study abroad program, with limited available funds we embraced a few students from different regions in Japan where there have been natural disasters to stay in Tokyo for a week. These were students who had lost family members and became refugees within their own country because of the disasters that devastated their lives. We wanted to give students who were living in temporary shelters or who have become orphans a chance to live a more colorful life. Their world might look bleak at the moment, but we wanted to give them the opportunity to have a brighter future. Each student was provided full scholarships to participate in the program.

The goal behind the Summer Program in Tokyo was to give eager and driven students the opportunity to broaden their world and give them the guidance and support they needed to build a career in the future. Through this program and activities, we hoped that students would be able to utilize their potential and see what they are truly capable of. The professional activities we had planned included: career coaching, workshops, visiting hotel sponsors to learn how the hospitality industry works, visiting watchmaking companies and their workshops, and attending Tokyo Children Summit on Environment hosted at the national government building. However, we also wanted to relate some of our activities to art and fashion, so we took the students to flower arrangement, pastry classes, fashion designer factories, and many more creative activities.

Summit on Environment, 2018

The following year, in 2020, we had planned on creating another summer program. It was our hope and idea to have this program annually, like our study abroad program. However, due to the global pandemic, we had to delay the program till it is possible for the children to travel and extend the program to the next level.

As part of this scheme, Okinawa was going to host the next summer program. With the same process, procedure, and mission as the Tokyo program, we wanted to give the youth an opportunity and chance to take off and flourish within their own life.

Our philosophy and objective of these programs was solely about soaking up as much knowledge as possible, it was to provide students who have faced hardship the tools to create a brighter and more colorful future.

Our vision was to give them hope, instill within them resilience, and hope that they walk away enlightened and empowered.

Encountering some severe changes in life at a young age was not easy for me. I was fortunate to have a supportive family and friends who encouraged me to continue on, keep faith, and have courage. However, not everyone has that in their life. It can be hard to keep your dreams and plan for a future when faced with unexpected hardships.

With the study abroad and Tokyo summer program, we wanted to give back to the next generation, paying forward all the hope and courage others had given me. The goal for these students is to learn more about the world we live in, the sacrifices other people have gone through, and how to be resilient, keep faith, hold onto hope, and be courageous even when hardship and struggling knocks you down. It is with this in mind that hopefully, one day, these children will grow into seasoned adults who are able to follow their aspirations and live a life that makes them fulfilled and grateful. In the future, maybe they would be able to pay forward all that they have learned and received.

Since the founding of RFH, there have been so many positive developments, additional sponsors, endorsements, and levels of success that we have reached. One of the biggest opportunities that came to RFH was mid-2019 when our foundation was officially endorsed and supported by Japan's Fashion Week organization. They offered us a large, national platform in Tokyo Fashion Week to participate and plan our runway show or related program during the fashion week in Spring and Fall each year. We were more than fortunate to be able to utilize their platform and expand the capabilities for RFH.

While this was a big step for the foundation, our progress and endorsements did not end there. After the backing of Japan's Fashion Week, we received an offer to organize events during Ginza Fashion Week in early 2020. The organization (Ginza Creative Salon) was associated with five major department stores/malls in Tokyo (Mitsukoshi, Matsuya, Ginza Six, Wako, and Tokyu Plaza) while Matsuya would host the main event. The opportunity provided to us was more than we had expected, and everyone was delighted by the support and chance to contribute. We wanted to do something truly unique and special, so we organized a children's runway show which was the most colorful event we ever hosted. The brilliance of the children was unforgettable.

In the years following the creation of RFH, our team has faced numerous struggles and obstacles on our path to success. However, with determination and unwavering dedication, we worked together to overcome these roadblocks and make it to the other side where a plethora of opportunities were waiting for us. Not only did we get to help those suffering from hardships and displacement within Japan, but we were able to give back to the next generation.

The younger generation holds the keys to our future. They are our aspiration for a better world, and by nurturing and paying forward what we have learned, we can only hope that they are brave and strong enough to make the change.

An extraordinary life filled with determination isn't just rising from the ashes of hardship and fighting to survive, it is *how* you live with the hardship and *what* you do to survive. Striving for a better future isn't about forgetting your past, it is about utilizing the things you have learned and the people who have helped you in your time of need in order to do better for yourself and for others. No one is born perfect. We all have imperfections that try to stop us in our life, but it is living in harmony with the differences within us that make an extraordinary life filled with determination.

Importance of Life Design - An Educational Stepping Stone

Purpose and Target:

- Improve understanding of the "World Within and Without" for each child, teaching them how we all have the power to overcome challenges.
- To support children and youth to be better prepared for life and enable them to build a brighter life/career for their future.
- Build appreciation for the importance of parents and family.
- Present families with a set of guidelines and continuous training that empower their relationship with their children and communities.

- Promote stronger communication, interaction, moral values, and racial and gender equality.
- Educate about leadership, life innovation, self-reliance and resilience.

After launching our Life Design program, we were approached by many different institutions, governmental organizations and local towns within Japan who were interested in implementing our program in junior high and high schools. The interest that we received was highly beneficial to the development of the program. We received advice on what is required to empower the youth and create opportunities for their future, and with the feedback we received, we were able to make our program even stronger.

Among some of the local towns that were interested in our program were a few in the Tohoku region that had been struck by the 2011 tsunami. Since 2017, Runway for Hope has been an active partner in supporting towns in the Tohoku region that had suffered from the terrible tsunami. With lectures, talk shows, and providing specific curriculum, we had hoped to help the towns that have been in disarray for many years even after the tsunami.

Though it was more difficult to implement Life Design among public schools in Japan due to regulations, our program was adopted by many private and international schools throughout the country. We were able to give students the tools to make their life more colorful. Allowing them room and creative freedom to explore their vision, showing them what it looks like to have hope, and giving them means to have courage.

Kamaishi City Compass Project 2017 - 2019

It wasn't just through our runway show or our study abroad programs that we created opportunities for the children that have lost families, hope, and have nowhere else to go, but through arts and design, we hoped to give these children the opportunity to create a brighter future. We assisted, encouraged, and attempted to hone the potential within them, while also nurturing their self-confidence. Children are the key to the well-being of humanity and the world, and to guide them in the right and bright direction is the only thing we can hope to give them.

Runway for Hope's mission is always growing. We seek to help children build their dreams and career, transforming and empowering their lives so that they might have a brighter future. The foundation strives to help the next generation be prepared and provide them with more opportunities to succeed in life. There will always be hardships and struggles in life, but with the right tools and knowledge, we hope that the youth will be able to overcome their complications and walk on a more colorful path to the future. We want to provide the youth the ability to build bridges, make strong connections, and nurture their vision so that one day, they might go out into the world and make a difference. *

Career Development

CONCLUSION

Our World Today

Everyday there is news about how humankind is pulling away from the common humanity that we all share. The dreams and vision, the hope and courage that drives us forward are swept away with chaos, regional and ethnic conflict, poverty gaps, the migration of people, and human violence. War and destruction seem to be ingrained into us as humans because it follows us throughout history; but if we take a step back and look at the overall spectrum of *why* conflict starts, we can see that it is because of our differences. What makes us unique and special as individuals, are what causes others to view us as a threat, and likewise, we see others as threats because of their differences.

The most challenging things our society and world will have to face today are *people* and *life itself.* There will come a point in our life where we will have to decide what is more important: our differences or our common humanity? Which one will we sacrifice to live a better life?

Many of us are living a life surrounded by technological advancements that are highly influenced by the thoughts of others. We can unlock a plethora of information at our fingertips that begin to forget the boundaries within the technological world. We feel powerful being anonymous online, knowledgeable by all the information we can gather, and connected to the world that we live in.

However, with the knowledge that we have access to, many people are starting to become more aware about global poverty, global warming, personal security, global epidemics, and other large issues that burden the world. It is alarming and terrifying that the world has become so advanced, yet problems such as these continue to lag behind. Despite the technology, what we do for others facing these problems is underwhelming, just as we feel overwhelmed by these problems.

If we live on a planet that houses over six billion people, half of them live on less than two dollars a day. While we struggle to make minimum wage, buy the house of our dreams, and secure our future, others are merely grateful for the opportunity to make less than what it costs us to buy a cup of coffee. There are billions more that live on less than a dollar a day. Even more that go to bed *hungry* every night or don't have access to *clean water*. Every hour 35 women die in *childbirth* and every half hour; a child *starves* to death.

It is overwhelming to hear about all the horrible things going on in the world. Most of us forget that we live in the Minority World, a world that is developed and where we have access to clean water, opportunities, and so on. However, in the Majority World, where most of the population resides, these statistics aren't surprising, though they might be overwhelming. The world we live in seems so different from the numbers and statistics provided to us that we can't fathom those things like this actually happen. Despite the knowledge we can attain through the use of technology, we refuse to believe that the world is as bad and as damaged as it actually is. We have our own problems and our own struggles, so why should we care?

Technology has given many societies power. We can do more than cheat, steal, and bully online, we have the power of helping and making a change in the world. Think about your personal security. We try our hardest to protect our security. We put our money in banks, we have a million passwords, we get home security, and we protect ourselves and our livelihoods at no small cost. However, no matter where we are in the world, whether we have financial means or if we are a part of the three billion people who struggle with global poverty, we are never *truly* safe.

Threats of state (physical torture), threats from other states (war), threats from other groups of people (ethnic tension), threats from individuals or organizations (crime, street violence, gangs), threats directed against women (rape, domestic violence), threats directed at children based on their dependence (child abuse), threats to self (suicide, drug use, etc.), there are threats everywhere. Perhaps we can't relate to the fact that a child dies of *starvation* every thirty minutes, but we can relate to the threats that impose on our lives. We know how it feels to want to be safe and scared when our safety is threatened. We share common needs and emotions, which is our common humanity.

Our differences put a gap between us, but it is our shared humanity that bridges that gap. Even if we cannot have empathy for those suffering differently than us, we can relate to the needs and desires every human has. There are basic ethics and foundations we need in order to be a compassionate and connected society. If we don't allow these foundations to take precedence over our differences, then we have doomed the future of humankind. Furthermore, if we cannot put aside our differences and bridge the gap between one another, then how are we supposed to take care of the world we live in?

CONCLUSION

Global warming is only getting worse, and yet society puts these issues on the back burner. This issue isn't new, it has been around for decades, yet the people in charge of this world don't care much since there is no monetary gain or interest to the lobbyist. With the rate our world is warming, we will lose island nations in the Pacific, coastal regions will be swallowed by the rising ocean, the South Pole and North Pole will grow smaller and many animals will go extinct. We are already seeing and feeling the consequences of global warming, yet many people still want to believe that the issue doesn't exist.

If we keep pretending that global warming doesn't exist, the suffering and injustice that is going on in the world will only grow. More people will become refugees, there will be more terror and violence and resources become tighter and the land becomes smaller. The differences that divide nations and create war will no longer exist because we will all be fighting for the same need for survival. However, if we could put our differences aside and respect that other people have different practices, backgrounds and religions than we do, then we can start working together to heal the world.

There are so many issues the world is facing. Perhaps there will never be a time in history where peace truly exists, however, we can always continue working towards a safer and more equal world where equity could thrive. Even though we have our own vision, our own dreams to nurture, our own hope and courage we need to focus on, we should never forget the world we live in. With technology at our disposal and knowledge easily accessible, we need to be prepared for the future and what world we want to leave behind for our children or for the generations to come.

CONCLUSION

"Human beings are members of a whole,
In creation of one essence and soul.
If one member is afflicted with pain,
Other members uneasy will remain.
If you've no sympathy for human pain,
The name of human you cannot retain!"

-Poem by Iranian poet Saadi, from the 13th century
Inscribed On United Nations Building Entrance, New York

While the world has progressed to the point that slavery, child labor, nuclear power, human sacrifice, etc., are not long socially acceptable, the violence and destruction has only evolved and adapted to different aspects of human life. With societal and technical advancements, the way we interact with the world and others begins to change. We stop listening to those around us, we complain about what we don't have and forget about what we do, we hurt each other and blame one another for problems we couldn't solve on our own, and we stop caring and having empathy for those who aren't as fortunate as us.

Most people in the Minority World are so occupied with life inside our little, materialistic bubble that we forget about the beauty within ourselves. We are preoccupied with wanting more out of life that we forget that what we have within our life is just as important as what is without. We all have the opportunity to flourish, thrive and listen to our values, but if we insist on only focusing on life outside of ourselves, then what makes us uniquely human will fade away.

That isn't to say that science and technology are the enemy of humankind and hinder our lives. However, with the quick technological advancements, we weren't given the time to balance our lives. Between being present and being sucked into our screens, we need to find a balance between our hunger for knowledge of the world and our connections to the people around us. Nurture the foundations of our family ties, communicate with friends more often, connect with our community and create a dialogue between the important pillars in our lives.

It is good to be curious and search for the answers to our questions using the tools and technology available to us. We first foster our vision and our dreams by being curious about the world, however, being too malleable by the ideas and thoughts we find can affect the way we connect with one another. Not every voice that comes into your life is a good director. Sometimes directors can lead you astray, make you lose faith in your dreams, or put you down when you need to be picked up. Dare to ask questions but question the answers you find. Everyone has their own bias, judgment, and thoughts. Trust those who are willing to support your vision and your dreams without changing who you are.

New Generation - Lead the Way and Transcend

Life is more important than the boxes we are put in and the boxes we put others in. While our identity is a part of our vision and our dream, it shouldn't be what distances us from one another. Our differences make us unique, and once we understand our differences and push aside our prejudice, we can live alongside harmony with our vision and dreams. The answer is easy to give, but harder to live.

On the other hand, with so much information available to us and the advancement of technology and communication the generations to come will be much more equipped in this quickly evolving society. The next generation are faced with the challenges of living in a fast-paced society that is easy to learn and constantly demanding more. Their lives are filled with different struggles and problems that their parents or grandparents were faced with, but they are struggles, nonetheless.

Generation Z and then Alpha, unarguably, will not only lead our future but make a huge mark on human evolution. What we have fought and lived for will shift with each, more technologically advanced generation. However, will hope and faith still be present? In the face of adversaries, challenges and struggles, will the next generation be able to have a sense of apathy for life and humankind? Will faith, morality, and the evolution of humankind and its role in history be something the next generation cares about? With a world of technology and knowledge unlocked, will they have to sacrifice one aspect of life for another? And lastly, will the next generation be able to create a better world, or will they destroy it?

There is always so much fear and uncertainty when something new appears in life. When technology advances, society broadens their vocabulary and inclusivity, when new achievements are accomplished, there is always hesitancy in accepting the new normal. However, despite all the fear and uncertainty, we need to have hope and give courage to those who will be leading the world next. Just as we were given direction, support, courage and hope, to lead our lives and our generation, we need to give the next generation the means to do better.

Educate the youth and guide them to the values in life, the ethics we build ourselves on, and show them that they can attain true happiness. By helping the next generation understand more about history and the inclusivity of the world, what humans have achieved, and how they ended up in this place in life will give them the foundation they need to make their own choices and decisions. As mothers, fathers, mentors, teachers, brothers or sisters, our job to help the youth attain a brighter, more colorful future is by guiding. Teach them about the struggles their ancestors or other people in history have gone through, the fight and struggle they had to endure for the chance of having opportunities.

Education is the most important ingredient to creating a brighter and better future. As the years go on, more and more children are being educated, but it still isn't enough. There are many places where women are not allowed to earn an education. The minority ethnic and those with lower socioeconomic life in the Minority World still struggle to receive education despite societal advancements. In the Majority World, poverty or diseases like AIDS prevent kids from having an education. More than 200 million kids around the world never receive an education.

Not every child has the blessing and benefits of a loving family, a decent home, the wealth or means to an education. We can't always make a difference in the lives of the children we want to help, but we need to try our best to make an impact on those we can reach. We need to be there for the children we mentor, teach, interact with, and raise. Everyone is going through something different, and the struggles we face aren't always the same, however, just by letting them know that we are there for them is enough sometimes.

If we can provide the youth with basic tools to move forward, follow their vision, never lose hope, and have courage to keep fighting, then the next generation will surely be able to build a life of color instead of one filled with destruction, violence, and selfishness. We were only able to have hope when the directors in our lives believed in us and gave us a reason to believe in ourselves. We had courage because we saw the hard work and sacrifices others in our lives have made. We fought for our vision because we had hope and courage, but even more so, we are able to attain our vision because of the people in our lives who made it possible.

Paying forward what we have learned throughout our journey is a task that we might spend our whole lives doing. Just as we are constantly chasing after many dreams or reminding ourselves to have hope or be courageous, we will constantly be finding ways to pay forward all the good we have received in our life.

The beauty of the world outside of gadgets and technology is something many of us take for granted. We live in a world so tethered to technology that we sometimes forget to look up and notice the brightness of a full moon, or the crisp yellow of autumn leaves. We forget to not only communicate with those around us, but the world around us as well. It is a habit most of us have to consciously overcome, however, it is a habit we shouldn't force onto the youth. Unplug the children in your life and have them take a moment to really appreciate the world. Lead by example and help them communicate with nature and their surroundings.

Some parents think that it is too late for change. Some believe that they don't have anything useful to share with their young ones or that communicating is something they aren't good at. However, it is without a doubt that parents have an enormous influence over their child and their child's life path. As a human and guardian to the next generation, we need to have the determination to create a strong connection with our children. It is our job to teach them and show them a whole world that they will have to navigate through. It doesn't matter what our background is, what skills we may or may not have, or our age, what matters is that we find common ground with our children.

Create games, talking points, and opportunities for your children to spend time with you. Quality time is important in any relationship, especially in a parent-child relationship. Find what you are good at and create a special bond with them rather than letting them walk all over you from a young age. Smile, hug, kiss, and tell your child that you love them. Be present when you are with them and your bond will strengthen.

What you have to teach the future generation matters. No matter what role children play in your life, remember that they are the voice of the future. They need the right guidance and compassion in order to succeed with the hopes and dreams of previous generations. However, being a good mentor for the youth isn't always easy. To build a stronger future, we need to reflect on ourselves, though most of us are too scared to look in the mirror. Children are sponges that soak up every atom around them. They learn from what we say and what we don't say, what we own up to and what we blame others for. If we cannot better ourselves, how can we trust our children to do better?

We need to learn more empathy and practice healthy dialogue more regularly. Instead of following the destructive path of history and falling into the ease of discriminating against others through the safety of a computer screen, we need to learn how to connect with those different from us. Unite as human beings and revel in the beauty of our differences. We aren't just robots programmed only to scorn and hate, we have the capability of changing and *making* changes in the world.

Most of us believe that our differences are what makes us important and gives our lives meaning. While our differences make each and every one of us unique, it also puts a wall between us and others. In some respects, our differences make us who we are, however, this shouldn't be the reason we cast aside our common humanity. If we are all different, then why are we fighting to be the same? The clash between being different and sharing a common humanity is what will define and shape the soul of new centuries. We should respect our differences and be kind to one another because we are all distinctly human. If we don't, the more advanced our societies become, the more damage the world endures.

Change isn't always easy and the mannerisms ingrained into us from our family, community, and schooling can be difficult and uncomfortable to challenge. Dare to go forth with an open mind and question the institutions you were brought up in. Sometimes the answers are what society makes them, and other times, you'll be surprised by the color you never knew existed. We need to approach our existence by reminding ourselves that we are human. Humans make mistakes and we aren't always perfect, but the beautiful thing about being human is that we grow and evolve. Remember our ancestors and the great lives they lived, what they gave, and how they cared and protected each other. Everyone has a story, but no one story is perfect. We are all striving towards a more colorful future, but the key is to be mindful of the world within as well as the world without. We can create the world of our dreams for our family and children, but since it's a world without walls, it will have to be a home for everyone, and we will call them family.

He who loves, lives; he who loves himself lives in hell; he who loves another lives on earth; he who loves others lives in heaven; but he who silently adores the true self of all creatures, lives in that self, and it is eternal peace.

-Ancient Hindu Philosopher

Reflect on yourself:

How can we build up the colors in our lives?

_____

_____

_____

_____

_____

_____

_____

_____

How will we be able to fulfill our vision with the opportunities we have available to us?

_____

_____

_____

_____

_____

_____

_____

_____

What do we need to do to make sure our hope is resolute, and our courage is strong?

_____
_____
_____
_____
_____
_____
_____
_____
_____

How will we be able to provide and pay forward the colors in our lives onto the next generations?

_____
_____
_____
_____
_____
_____
_____
_____
_____

COGNITIVE ACTIVITY
Thoughts and Action Plan

- Explore ideas

- Discover new interests and reconnect

- Physical exercise & peaceful walking

- Think of what makes you happy and alive everyday

- Write down your smallest dream

- Then the biggest dream

- Put down your goals (5 years, 10 years, 20 years, retirement)

COGNITIVE ACTIVITY

SELF DEVELOPMENT – CORE VALUES

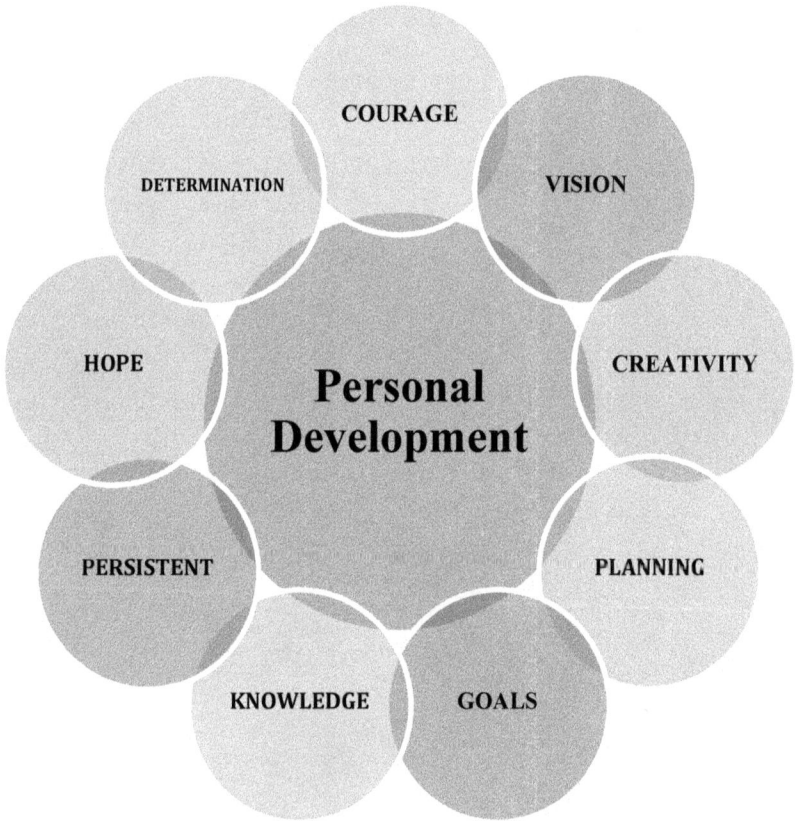

COURAGE

DETERMINATION

VISION

HOPE

Personal Development

CREATIVITY

PERSISTENT

PLANNING

KNOWLEDGE

GOALS

WORLD WITHIN – CORE VALUES

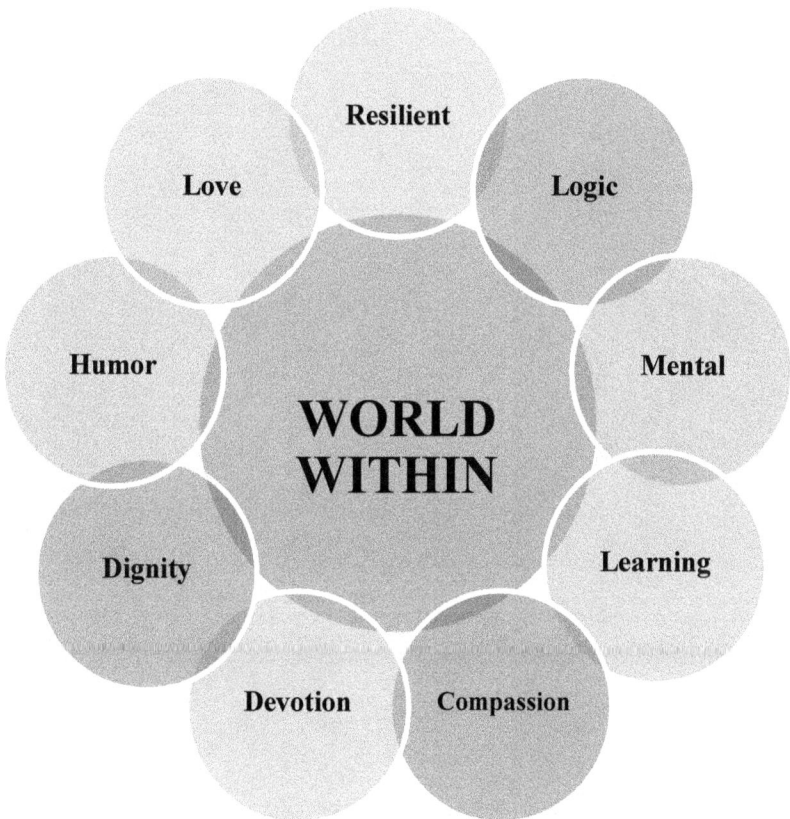

www.ingramcontent.com/pod-product-compliance
Lightning Source LLC
Chambersburg PA
CBHW072058020426
42334CB00017B/1556